Green's Cuisine

Green's Cuisine

Low Fat Food with a Taste of Thailand

by
Daniel Green

To Eleanor with love

Acknowledgment

The author and the publisher thank the Bangkok Marriott Resort and Spa for the facilities they provided during the preparation of this book.

ISBN 974-7248-79-4

Copyright © 2003

Published in Thailand by
Book Promotion and Service Company Limited
2220/31 Ramkhamhaeng 36/1
Huamark, Bangkok 10240
Thailand
Tel: 66 2 7320243-5
Fax: 66 2 3752669
E-mail: publishing@book.co.th

Distributed by
Booknet Company Limited
1173, 1175, 1177, 1179 Srinakharin Road
Suan Luang, Bangkok 10250
Thailand
Tel: 66 2 3223678
Fax: 66 2 7211639
E-mail: booknet@book.co.th

Author: Daniel Green
www.televisioncookery.com

Photographs: Thewin Chanyawong
www.photoessay@hotmail.com

Design: Pimmas Suksri

Printed and bound in Thailand by
Amarin Printing & Publishing Public Company Limited

All rights reserved. No part of this publication may be reproduced, stored in a retrieval system, or transmitted in any form or by any means, electronic, mechanical, photocopying, recording or otherwise, without the prior permission of the publisher.

Contents

My Story ...

This book is special to me as I had to struggle to lose weight. I shed over 28 kilogrammes and have stayed slim for over nine years now. I lost weight over a period of three years and always stress the importance of shedding those extra kilos slowly. There are too many diets that get the weight off so fast that it is impossible to sustain. I lost kilos on a low fat regime but the difference was I loved food and did not want to deprive myself of my favourite meals and treats. So I decided I would adapt my favourite food to a low fat healthy alternative. This worked for me and while I was dieting I devised some great recipes. You will find many of them in this book. After losing weight I became a model and had a successful career enabling me to travel the world. But at heart, I wanted to follow my passion: cookery.

I now have a career as a writer and in television cookery where I get to demonstrate my techniques and ideas to viewers all over the world. I have had a series on the Carlton Food Network as well as filming special programmes for many other networks. I have also had a series in Asia and much of my inspiration comes from that part of the world.

The Method ...

I want this book to give motivation and determination for people to lose weight. It is not an easy task so that is why, through my recipes, I am trying to make it fun and exciting. We have all seen low fat cookbooks. But how many of them are inspirational? We do not want yet another baked potato with cottage cheese recipe or more bland pastas. So I have created food that is modern in style that would not be out of place in a stylish London restaurant. I love the idea of fusion food and British modern food, so why not make it low fat? So I take ingredients and flavours, old and new recipes from different parts of the world and adapt them to low fat cuisine. For example, I make a fat free curry. It's not exactly the same taste as the original but it provides options for every day eating.

Diets do not work. Why? Because they restrict you; they tell you never touch this or that. What does this create? Bingeing. My way is to eat sensibly and well every day with time off for a little indulgence now and again. I love cheese. It's my weakness. So occasionally I will not restrict how much I eat. I know I will not put on weight by letting go every now and again. You can do the same. If you are going out for a special meal, enjoy yourself. Don't feel guilty that you're eating a fried steak followed by a creamy dessert. You will gain confidence knowing that you can enjoy an indulgent day out and still eat well during the rest of the week on my low fat taste-of-the-orient recipes.

Recently, the trend in dieting has been to eat protein only, cutting out carbohydrates. You cannot ignore such a vital food type from your diet as it will create a craving for starchy foods. That's why when people come off these diets they put on all the weight they lost, and more.

The Food ...

This is how it works. Food must be exciting and tasty. With my recipes you will be able to enjoy all your favourite foods and lose weight. I have designed recipes from Italian to Thai and have adapted each so that they are very low in fat. Although I am cutting out the fat I am replacing it with the powerful and wonderful flavours of fresh herbs and Asian spices. I use coriander, basil, lemongrass and many more. To ensure you are using the freshest ingredients you need to go to the supermarket a few times a week. This may not seem ideal but you need the fresh vegetables, fruit and herbs to make great low fat food. You'll also reduce your weekly bills if you shop every two or three days because you won't be throwing out expired goods. You will also not be overeating to stop food going past its expiry date!

The reason I love making my recipes for houseguests is because many people are careful in what they eat. If I make something with a little more fat than usual, I do it as an option because everything else will be low fat. These days many people are relieved to find their host has prepared a healthy meal. There is nothing worse that eating fattening food when you have decided you do not want to.

Lastly, what makes my food different from others in the healthy eating category? I present food in a spectacular way. I do this even when cooking for myself. Why?...you may think. Well, to begin with, if you sit down to a meal that looks like it's from the kitchens of a top restaurant, you'll forget it's low fat. So think of my food as coming from your favourite restaurant or cookbook which by the way, happens to be low fat.

Bon appetite!

CANAPES

Tuna and Olive Canapes

Smoked White Fish Blinis

Salmon with Olive and Anchovy Tapenade

Crab and Spinach Canapes

Tuna and Olive Canapes

Preparation time: 5-7 minutes

I make this a day prior to serving as the flavours really mature overnight.

1	can tuna in brine
1	clove garlic
	Juice of 1 lemon
2	teaspoons capers
1	heaped teaspoon dijon mustard
¾	large tin pitted black olives
1	ciabbate or french loaf

Place the ingredients in a blender and mix to a paste. Keep in the fridge until ready to serve. Grill the sliced bread until brown on each side then top with the paté.

Smoked White Fish Blinis

Preparation & cooking time: 15 minutes
Serves 4

I make this dish when I am not sure what my guests like as it seems that everyone enjoys this recipe.

100g (3.5 oz.) smoked white fish
1 egg
110ml (4 fl.oz.) milk
30g (1 oz.) flour
4 tablespoons fat free fromage frais or plain yoghurt
4 spring onions
Fresh chives

Sieve the flour into a bowl, add the egg and milk and whisk together making a pancake batter. Make sure this mixture is not too sloppy.

Heat a non stick frying pan and fry separately, four spoonfuls of batter, each about two inches in diameter. When you have made three for each guest, put onto a plate. Chop the spring onions and put in the middle of the plate then add the smoked fish on the pancakes. Place a spoonful of fromage frais or yoghurt at the end of the plate and put two chives crossing each other on each pancake.

Salmon with Olive and Anchovy Tapenade

Preparation & cooking time: 40 minutes
Serves 4

This is another excellent main course for entertaining.
I serve it on a ring of mashed potatoes but it is equally good with a ring of spinach.

4	salmon fillets, skinned
1	can black pitted olives
½	can anchovies, drained
2	teaspoons capers
	Juice of 1 lemon
500g	(1 lb.) spinach
2	teaspoons sesame oil
2	teaspoons soy sauce

Take the olives, lemon juice, capers and anchovies and mix in a blender to make the tapenade. Place the salmon fillets on a baking tray. With a teaspoon take the tapenade and neatly make a crust over the salmon. Place in a fan assisted oven on 180°-190°C (200°-220°C regular oven) for 18-20 minutes. When almost ready, put the spinach in a saucepan with a touch of water, add the sesame oil and soy sauce and let the spinach reduce in size. Make a bed of spinach on a plate and place the salmon on top. If you prefer potatoes, peel, boil, season and mash some potatoes and make into a ring.

Crab and Spinach Canapes

Preparation time: 15 minutes
Serves 12-15

I love doing canapes as you can fit in so many flavours for a three course dinner party.
This one is fat free and full of flavour.

1	loaf french bread
225g	(½ lb.) spinach
1	tin white crab meat or 200g (7 oz.) Fresh crab meat
1	red chilli finely chopped
	Dash of tabasco
	Salt and pepper

All you do is slice the loaf into 1 inch slices then toast. Blanch the spinach in boiling water for 3-4 minutes and drain. In a bowl mix together the spinach, chilli, tabasco, salt, pepper and the crab meat.

Evenly place some of the mixture on each slice of toasted french bread and serve all together on a large plate.

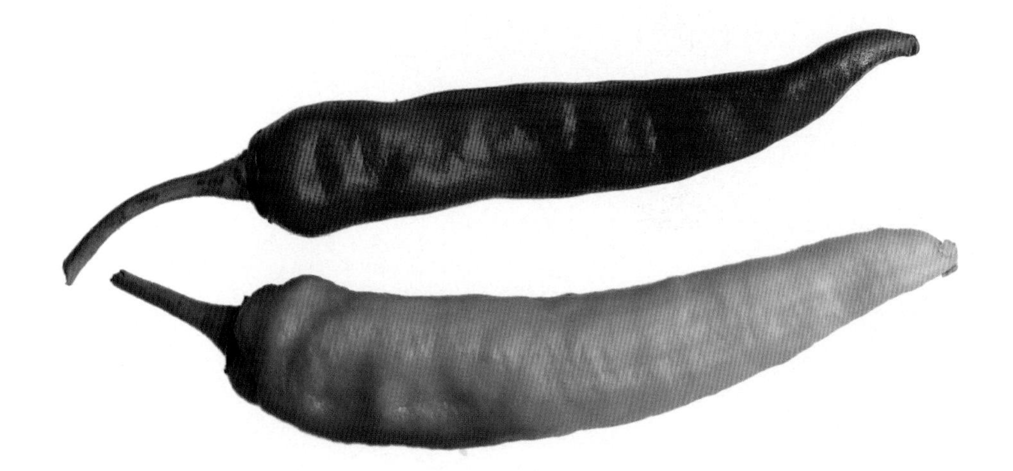

STARTERS

Greek Party Dip

Bruschetta

Thai Garlic Bread

Pea Pancakes with Smoked Salmon

Smoked Salmon Creamed Rings

Salmon Wrapped in Parma Ham Salad

Smoked Salmon with Quail Eggs and Salmon Eggs

Baked Garlic with White Fish and Lemongrass Paté

Trout Paté

Spanish Tapas : Tomato Mussels

Spanish Tapas : Red Peppers and Anchovy

Spanish Tapas : Asparagus in Parma Ham with Quail Eggs

Breadsticks with Tomato Sauce

Stuffed Red Peppers

Stuffed Thai Peppers

Greek Party Dip

Preparation & cooking time: 15 minutes

I wish I could call this low fat. But on the other hand it is not high in fat and has fresh, healthy ingredients. It is such a simple dish. Your guests will love it. It's also a great starter to make if you are cooking a complicated dish as an entree that requires a little more time.

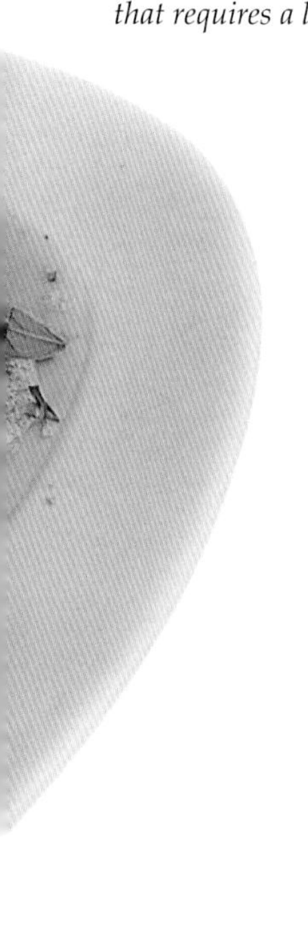

1 pack feta cheese
600g (1¼ lb.) cherry tomatoes
5 tablespoons olive oil
Large handful of fresh basil leaves
Loaf of warm bread

Take a large wok or frying pan and add the olive oil. Halve the cherry tomatoes and add to the pan. Turn on the heat. The reason you do not start by heating the oil is because the tomatoes must cook gently. On a low heat cook for 6-10 minutes or until they look like they are about to collapse. Crumble the feta cheese and add to the pan. Stir well and cook for another few minutes. You want to keep this dish nice and chunky. Slice up the basil, throw in the pan and take off the heat. Stir and transfer to a large serving dish. Serve with your favourite bread to mop up the juices.

If you have any left over which is unlikely, keep in the refrigerator and use as a pasta sauce.

Bruschetta

Preparation & cooking time: 10 minutes
Serves 4

This is great served as a canape or you can place a few on a plate for a starter.

1	ciabatta loaf or french bread
1	large onion finely chopped
	Bunch fresh coriander leaves
8	medium tomatoes, deseeded
1	clove crushed garlic
	Juice of 1 lime or ½ a lemon
I	tablespoon olive oil

In a large frying pan heat the oil then add the garlic and finely chopped onion. Let them sweat over a medium heat for about 3-5 minutes stirring continuously. Then add the tomatoes and lemon juice. Leave on a low heat for about 10 minutes and then cool. Shred the basil and add to the pan. This mixture does not have to be served hot. Room temperature is fine.

When you are ready to serve, cut the ciabatta loaf into two inch slices and grill each side until golden, or pop into a toaster oven. Place a large spoonful of sauce on each slice and serve.

Thai Garlic Bread

Preparation & cooking time: 20 minutes
Serves 4

Garlic bread is a very western dish but I have adapted it using Thai herbs and spices to make a great side dish to a soup or starter. It's really easy to make so give it a try.

1	french loaf or ciabatta bread
3	cloves garlic
3	lemongrass stalks
1	teaspoon freshly grated ginger
1	red chilli
1	tablespoon olive oil
1	tablespoon sesame oil
1	lime
	Large handful fresh coriander leaves

Cut the bread in half lengthways. In a blender (or you can chop very finely by hand) add all the above ingredients. With the lime you can add the zest of the skin to give a little more flavour. If you do not have sesame oil you can use 2 tablespoons of olive oil.

Spread the mixture evenly on the bread. You can use a pastry brush if you want just a thin layer of spread.

You can cook this two ways. The first way is to place the coated halves of bread back together and wrap in foil. Cook in a fan assisted oven at 190°C (210°regular oven) or gas mark 6 for 10-12 minutes. The other way is to grill the bread on a barbecue for just a few minutes each side.

Pea Pancakes with Smoked Salmon

Preparation & cooking time: 15 minutes
Serves 4

This is a great starter and the peas in the batter make such a fantastic combination.

200g (7 oz.) smoked salmon
200g (7 oz.) fresh or frozen peas
1 egg
100ml (3.5 fl.oz) milk
75g (3 oz.) flour
Chives
6 tablespoons fromage frais or plain yoghurt
1 tablespoon creamed horseradish

In a bowl mix together the fromage frais or yoghurt and creamed horseradish and set aside.

Next, make the pancake batter. It should not be too thin nor too thick - in between a french crepe batter and an American pancake batter. Mix the flour, milk and egg to form the batter.

Steam the peas for about 5 minutes and place in a bowl. With a potato masher crush the peas so they are roughly mashed and add to the pancake batter.

In a frying pan (preferably a pancake pan) heat a drop of oil and wait until smoking. Reduce the heat and add a tablespoon of batter . You can probably make three at a time. When small bubbles appear on the top of each pancake flip them and cook the other side for about 30 seconds. You will probably find the first batch you make never turn out as well as the rest. I think this is because it takes a while to get the temperature right on the pan.

On a serving plate place three pancakes putting smoked salmon on each. Add two chives crossing each other on top of each. With two spoons make a quenelle with your fromage frais mixture by taking one spoonful of the mixture and taking it off one spoon with the other spoon. You can do this a few times to get the shape right.

Place the quenelle at the end of the plate. Serve.

Smoked Salmon Creamed Rings

Preparation time: 15 minutes
Serves 4

A fantastic starter that accompanies any dish perfectly and looks terrific. It's also so easy to make.

60g (2 oz.) smoked salmon
1 cucumber
10-15 radishes
6 tablespoons fat free fromage frais or plain yoghurt
1 teaspoon creamed horseradish
Fresh dill

Cut the cucumber in half and with a teaspoon run through removing and discarding the soft centre. Cut cucumber into very fine strips and place in a bowl. Slice the radishes into fine strips, chop some dill and add to the bowl along with the fromage frais and creamed horseradish. Mix well. Cut the smoked salmon into fine strips and add to the rest of the ingredients. When ready to serve, place a small pastry ring on each plate, fill with the mixture and lift off. I chop some dill to sprinkle around the edge of the plate to make this look spectacular.

Salmon Wrapped in Parma Ham Salad

Preparation & cooking time: 25-35 minutes
Serves 4

4 salmon fillets
8 slices parma ham

For salad:
2 large bags of mixed salad leaves or 2 cos lettuce
Olives
4-6 sun dried tomatoes
10-12 cherry tomatoes
4 spring onions
1 lemon
2 teaspoons dijon mustard
4 tablespoons olive oil

Wrap each salmon fillet in 2 slices of parma ham so that they are completely sealed. Place on a baking tray in a preheated fan assisted oven at 200°C (220°C regular) or gas mark 6 and cook for 16-18 minutes.

Meanwhile in a large bowl add all the salad ingredients. When you are nearly ready to serve, mix the juice of the lemon, mustard and olive oil and dress the salad. Serve the salad in individual portions accompanied by the salmon.

Smoked Salmon with Quail Eggs and Salmon Eggs

Preparation time: 15 minutes
Serves 4

If you are in a hurry and want a beautiful looking starter that is low in fat, make this.

450g (1lb.) smoked salmon
8-12 quail eggs
60g (2½ oz.) salmon eggs

Place the quail eggs in a pan with water to cover. Bring to the boil and leave for 3 minutes. Place in cold water and peel.

Divide the salmon onto four plates and then divide the salmon eggs and place in the middle of each dish. Cut the quail eggs in half and place around the salmon. Serve with large lemon wedges and enjoy.

Baked Garlic with White Fish and Lemongrass Paté

Preparation & cooking time: 40-45 minutes
Serves 4-6

450g (1 lb.) white fish (cod is a good choice)
100g (3½ oz.) low fat cream cheese
100g (3½ oz.) low fat plain yoghurt
2 lemongrass stalks
2 garlic bulbs

Here's a very simple dish that works well spread on thick crusty bread. Serve with a salad for a lunch meal or have as an hors d'oeuvre.

Place fish in a pan with water that just covers it. Bring to the boil and remove from heat covering with a lid. Leave for 15 minutes then drain and place in a bowl.

Meanwhile heat a fan assisted oven to 190°C (210°C regular) or gas mark 6. Cut the garlic bulbs in half, place them in silver foil, drizzle olive oil over them and place the halves back together. Cover in foil completely and bake for 40 minutes.

Remove hard outer layers of the lemongrass and then finely chop the rest adding it to the fish, followed by the yoghurt and cream cheese. Mix well or even place in a blender.

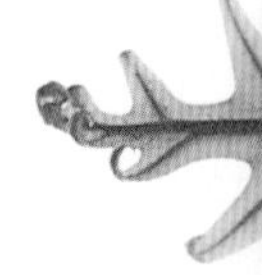

Remove garlic from the oven and spread a clove on the bread followed by some fish paté. You will find that as the garlic has cooked for so long it is no longer pungent and has a much more subtle flavour than raw garlic.

If you like a bit of a kick to your paté add a little red chilli.

Trout Paté

Preparation & cooking time: 18 minutes
Serves 4

175g	(6 oz.) low fat cream cheese
1	trout
1	french loaf
4	spring onions
½	teaspoon paprika
	Handful fresh basil
½	lemon
1	garlic clove
	Few parsley sprigs
1	tablespoon olive oil

This makes a lovely summer lunch or it is perfect before a barbecue. If you can't get trout, use any fish you like. When you buy the cream cheese make sure you look for the lowest in fat as most supermarkets now carry some very low fat varieties.

Place the trout in a pan and just cover with water. Add a few peppercorns and a bay leaf and bring to the boil. Simmer on a very gentle heat for 5-6 minutes. Remove from heat but let the fish stand in the pan for another 5 minutes.

Next, put the trout on a board and remove its skin. It will peel away easily. Remove the head and bones. Be careful, as trout has very fine bones and you do not want to have any in your paté.

Place the fish in a bowl and mix in the cream cheese with a fork. Slice the spring onions and add to the bowl followed by the juice of the lemon and the paprika. Roll up the basil leaves and slice adding them to the bowl. Combine all the ingredients well.

In a mortar and pestle crush the garlic and parsley with olive oil until you have a paste. Cut the bread in half and spread the paté. Serve two slices of the garlic bread followed by 2 spoonfuls of paté served in a quenelle shape.

Spanish Tapas : Tomato Mussels

Preparation & cooking time: 20 minutes
Serves 4

600g (1¼ lb.) mussels
600g (1¼ lb.) tomatoes
2 garlic cloves
3 tablespoons olive oil
1 red pepper deseeded

After spending a week filming in Spain I fell in love with tapas and just have to recreate for you some great dishes I had.

Slice the pepper and dice the tomatoes. Throw together into a large pan with the olive oil and garlic. Cook on a low heat for 15 minutes.

Remove from the heat and put into a blender until smooth. Return to the pan and gently simmer for another 5 minutes while you are cooking your mussels.

Steam the mussels over a pan of boiling water. This should take a few minutes. Discard any that don't open.

Remove one half of each shell leaving the half shell with the mussel in place. Serve a generous spoonful of the tomato sauce onto a plate where you have placed a few mussels.

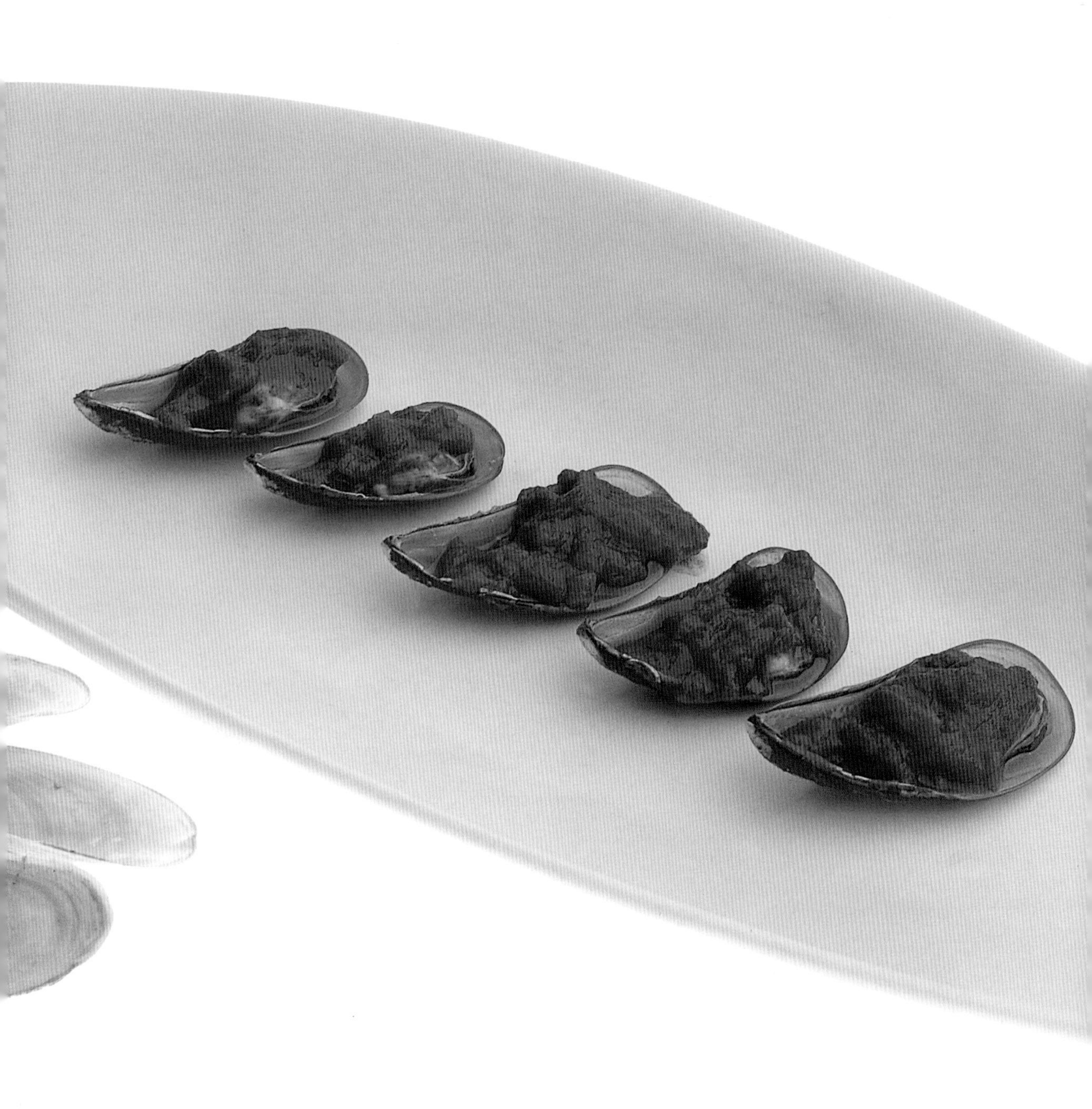

Spanish Tapas : Red Peppers and Anchovy

Preparation & cooking time: 50 minutes
Makes 12 tapas

A real Spanish classic tapas.

1	can anchovies
2	red peppers
2	garlic cloves
3	tablespoons olive oil
	French bread or ciabatta bread

Heat a fan assisted oven to 190°C (210°C regular) gas mark 6. Bake the peppers whole for 30-40 minutes. You want the skin to go black. Remove the peppers and immediately place in a plastic bag. Give the bag a good shake and remove the peppers. Their skin will fall off or be very easy to peel. Once you have peeled the pepper remove the stalk and seeds. Cut the peppers into 8 strips each. Place in a bowl with the olive oil and crushed garlic. You can make this way ahead of time or prepare a large batch to keep in the fridge.

Cut the bread into one inch slices. Add one or two slices of pepper followed by an anchovy fillet. Season and serve.

Spanish Tapas : Asparagus in Parma Ham with Quail Eggs

Preparation & cooking time: 12-15 minutes
Serves 4

12	large asparagus
12	slices parma ham
2	packs (12 quail eggs)

You can't get fewer ingredients than this but it looks great, tastes great and is perfect for Tapas.

All you do is boil a large pan of water. Before throwing in the asparagus just bend the end of each and where it snaps off is the part you want to discard as it's too tough. Boil the asparagus for 3-5 minutes. Drain and quickly soak in cold water to fix the colour.

Wrap a slice of parma ham around each asparagus. I peel off the fat from the ham just to make it more healthy. In another pan add the eggs, bring to the boil and cook for 5 minutes. Drain and remove the shells.

Serve all of the asparagus on a plate at one end with the quail eggs at the other.

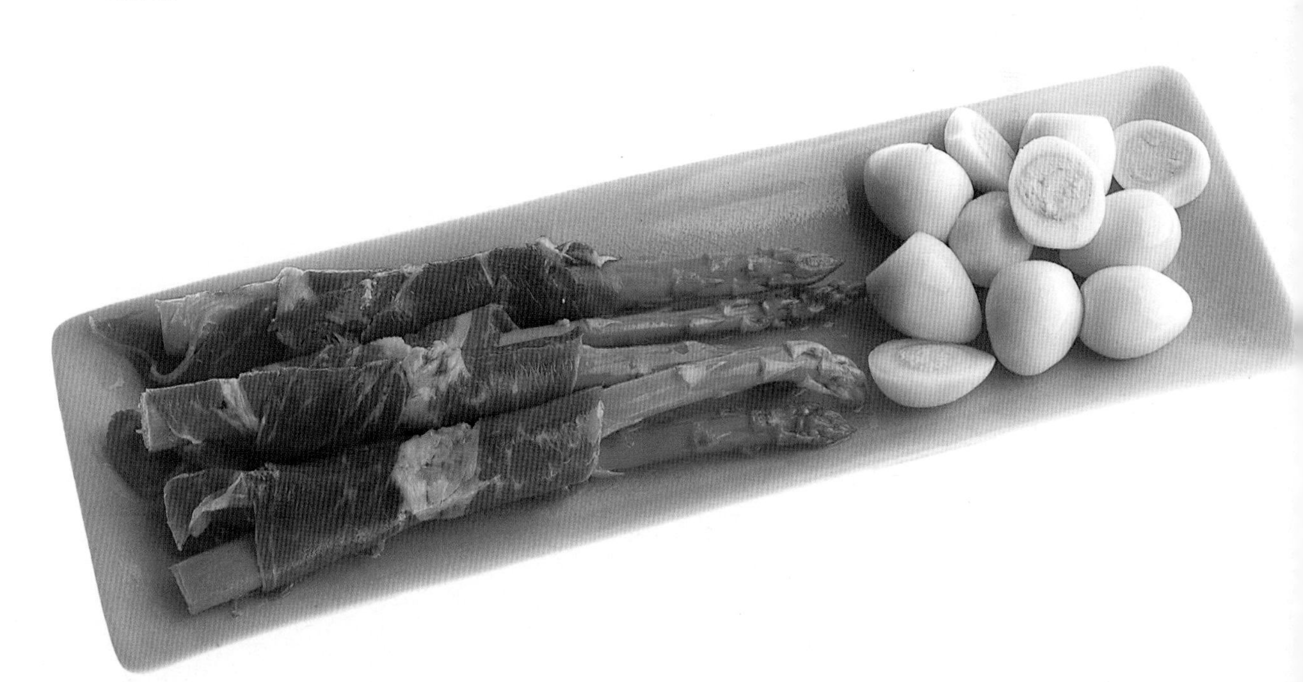

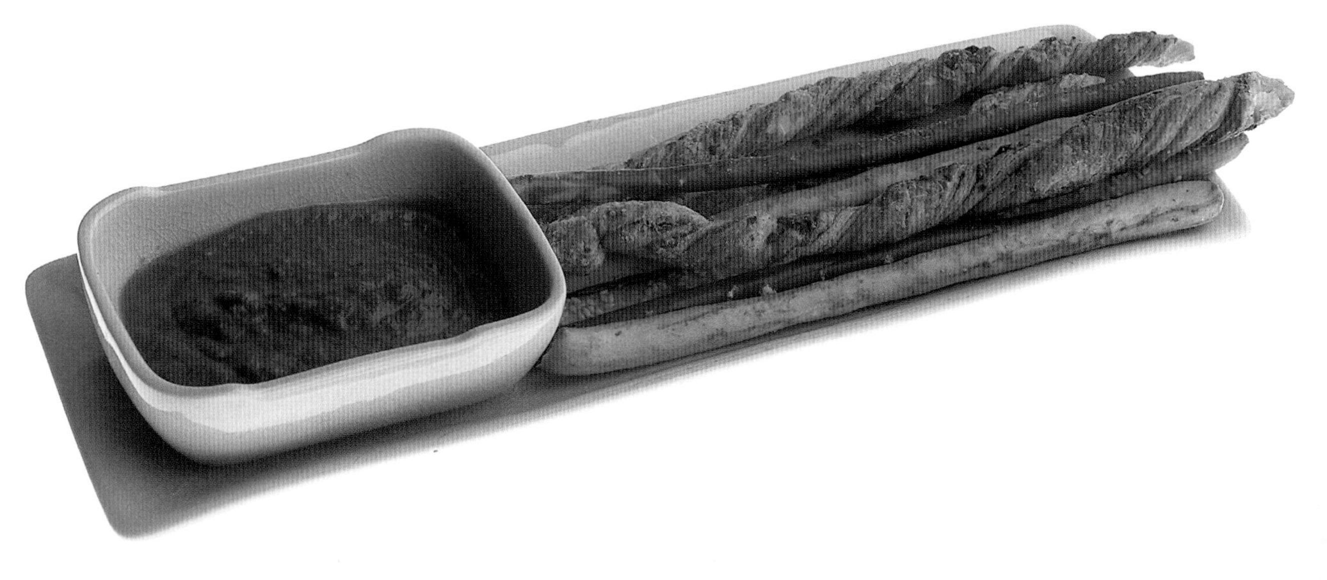

Breadsticks with Tomato Sauce

Preparation & cooking time: 6 minutes
Serves 4

This makes a great alternative to fattening crisps and snacks and works well for a dinner party with cocktails.

1 can tomatoes
1 clove garlic
3 tablespoons olive oil
1 tablespoon balsamic vinegar
Breadsticks to serve

In a pan heat a tablespoon of oil and crush and fry the garlic. After a few minutes add the tomatoes and the remaining oil and cook on a low heat for 5 minutes. Remove from the heat and blend in the vinegar.

Serve with breadsticks.

Stuffed Red Peppers

Preparation & cooking time: 70 minutes
Serves 6

3	red peppers (capsicum)
1	tablespoon capers
185g	(6.5 oz.) can tuna in brine or water
1	clove crushed garlic
50g	(1.5 oz.) can anchovy fillets
	Fresh basil leaves

This is a great starter that you can make a few hours ahead of your guests arrival and serve at room temperature.

Slice the peppers in half lengthways and if you can, keep the stalks on, cutting through them half way too.

Remove the seeds. Place peppers on a baking tray. Heat a fan assisted oven to 190°C (210°C regular) or gas mark 6 and start on the filling.

In a bowl mix together the tuna, capers and garlic. Distribute the mixture into all the pepper halves and chop the anchovy fillets adding them evenly to the peppers. If you wish you can drizzle the oil from the anchovy can onto the peppers to help the cooking process but remember it will have more fat.

Bake the peppers 25-30 minutes, remove from the oven and tear some basil leaves over each of them. They are now ready to serve.

You will find the peppers give a lot of juice so I suggest you serve this with some thick crusty bread to mop it up.

Stuffed Thai Peppers

Preparation & cooking time: 40 minutes
Serves 4-6

This is like fusion as peppers are used so much in the west and here they are mixed with Thai herbs and spices. This is a great starter or lunch option. This dish is also fat free

8 small green peppers (capsicums)

Filling

225g (8 oz.) fresh button or shitake mushrooms, chopped
2 tablespoons spring onions, chopped
1 tablespoon garlic, chopped
½ teaspoon ginger, chopped
¼ teaspoon pepper
¼ teaspoon sugar - optional
½ tablespoon cornstarch dissolved in 1 tablespoon water

Cut the tops off the peppers, remove seeds and set aside. Mix together thoroughly all the filling ingredients and stuff into the peppers. Place peppers in a shallow baking dish in a preheated fan assisted oven at 180°C (200°C regular) or gas mark 6 for 30 minutes. Or, steam over a high heat for 30 minutes. Before serving, brush the peppers with oil to make them shine (optional). Serve hot or at room temperature.

SOUPS, SALADS AND VEGETABLES

Parsnip and Sweet Potato Soup

Preparation & cooking time 35 minutes
Serves 6-8

This soup tastes so rich that you cannot believe there is no added cream.

6 parsnips
1 large sweet potato (white or orange)
1 onion
1 tablespoon olive oil
600ml (1 pint) milk (any can be used, I prefer skimmed milk)
900ml (1½ pints) vegetable stock
Chives

Dice four slices of white bread into cubes. Place in an oven dish and drizzle with olive oil. Mix croutons well and bake in a fan assisted oven at 190°C (210°C regular oven) or gas mark 6 for 10 minutes.

Peel the sweet potato and the parsnips and cut into chunks. Peel the onion and cut into quarters.

In a large saucepan heat the oil and throw in the onion, taking care not to brown it. After a minute add the sweet potato and parsnips. Fry for 3 minutes then add the stock and stir well. Once boiling turn the heat down and add the milk, then simmer for 25 minutes.

When ready, place a hand blender in the saucepan and blend thoroughly or use a food processor.

To serve, ladle the soup into bowls, add a few croutons and sprinkle with chopped chives.

Chicken Soup with Lemongrass

Preparation & cooking time: 25 minutes
Serves 4

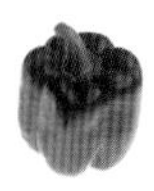

I love making large amounts of soup on a winters day and this is a perfect example. Traditionally this dish contains coconut milk. I have adapted this to stock and I really feel you get the same result. Eat as much as you want as it's low in calories and fat.

1 lemongrass stalk
4 lime leaves
2.5cm (1 in.) piece ginger
250g (8 oz.) shitake mushrooms
2 tomatoes
1-2 teaspoons chilli paste
450g (1 lb.) chicken fillets, no skin
400ml (13 fl.oz.) vegetable or chicken stock
4 tablespoons lemon juice
4 tablespoons fish sauce

Cut the lemongrass into 2.5cm (1 in.) pieces, fold lime leaves, wash ginger and slice finely. Cut mushrooms into halves. Chop the tomatoes. Slice chicken fillets.

Heat the stock and add the lemongrass. Simmer for two minutes. Pour in ¾ litre (1¼ pt.) water and heat. Add chicken, lime leaves, mushrooms and tomatoes and simmer for five minutes.

Season with chilli paste, fish sauce and lemon juice. Remove lemongrass and lime leaves before serving .

Tom Yum Goong

Preparation & cooking time: 20 minutes
Serves 4

This is truly my favourite Thai dish and can never be too hot for me. I have had this in many countries but never as good as in Thailand. For me the fresh lime leaves make the dish. The way to make this fat free is not to use any oil, and if using chicken, remove the skin. These are such little adaptations but they make the difference in fat content. This is also such an easy, quick recipe.

2 or 3	lemongrass stalks, finely chopped
900g	(2 lb.) tiger prawns or boneless chicken meat
5 or 6	kaffir lime leaves
	Lemon juice
	Fish sauce
3 or 4	red/green chillies
225g	(8 oz.) chinese mushrooms
1½	teaspoons Thai chilli paste
	Handful coriander leaves
	Water (half of the pot) in a 1.5 qt sauce pan.

Put the lemongrass and chilli paste in a pan. Throw in the prawns and mushrooms and boil for 10 minutes. Add the lime leaves and sliced chilli peppers. Cook for one minute. It's done! Now you can mix it in a serving bowl with lemon juice and fish sauce. Garnish with coriander and serve hot with Thai Jasmine rice.

Avocado Soup with Poached Salmon

Preparation & cooking time: 15 minutes
Serves 4

2 avocados
900ml (1½ pints) vegetable or chicken stock
2 salmon fillets
2 tablespoons low fat plain yoghurt
50g (2 oz.) salmon roe (optional)

To make the soup, whiz in a blender until smooth the avocados, stock and yoghurt. Meanwhile place the salmon in a pan of water, bring to the boil then remove and stand for 10 minutes.

Spoon some soup into a large bowl followed by half a salmon fillet and then top with some salmon eggs.

Great with Thai garlic bread.

Fresh Tuna Nicoise

Preparation & cooking time: 25 minutes
Serves 4

This is a stunning looking dish when presented correctly. By buying the tail end of tuna you'll give a perfect round shape to the dish. It also looks like it has been prepared by a top restaurant.

	Tail end of tuna (enough to be cut into three to five 5cm. (2 in.) slices per person)
12	new potatoes
30	french beans (approx.)
1	can pitted black olives
4	tablespoons olive oil
2	teaspoons dijon mustard
8	quail eggs or 4 chicken eggs
3	tablespoons lemon juice
2	cloves garlic

Start by placing the new unpeeled potatoes in an oven dish and add a little olive oil, plenty of salt and pepper and 2 cloves of crushed garlic. Mix together. Place in a 190°C fan assisted oven (210°C regular) or gas mark 6 for 20-30 minutes stirring the potatoes once or twice.

Boil the French beans for 5 minutes and immediately rinse under the cold tap to keep their colour. Set aside.

Boil the quail eggs for a few minutes. Shell them when cool.

In a blender or hand held blender, make the tapenade by whizzing the olives, half the lemon juice and a small clove of garlic.

For the dressing, mix together four tablespoons of olive oil, two teaspoons dijon mustard and the remaining lemon juice.

In a pan, add a tiny amount of olive oil and when hot, fry the tuna in one piece for about 15 seconds on each side. Remove from the pan. Slice the tuna into 2 inch wheels and place three to five pieces on each plate. Around the tuna add a few potatoes, halved quail eggs, dressed beans and a quenelle of the tapenade.

Bean and Mozzarella Salad

Preparation & cooking time: 8 minutes
Serves 4

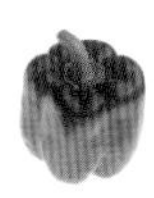

What an easy dish to make and it can be made ahead of time. This salad is perfect on a summer's day accompanied with bread to mop up the juices. Mozzarella does contain fat but it is one of the least fat cheeses around. Remember, with cheese the harder it is the more fat it contains with the exception of reduced fat cheese.

1	mozzarella ball, around 100g
1	can chick peas
1	can red kidney beans
1	can butter beans
2	tablespoons olive oil
	Handful fresh basil leaves
	Juice of 1 lemon
1	clove crushed garlic

Drain all the beans and mix well in a large bowl. Add the lemon juice, garlic and olive oil and mix well. Cut the mozzarella into small cubes and add to the bowl. Shred the basil and mix with the salad. Keep in the fridge overnight for all the flavours to intensify.

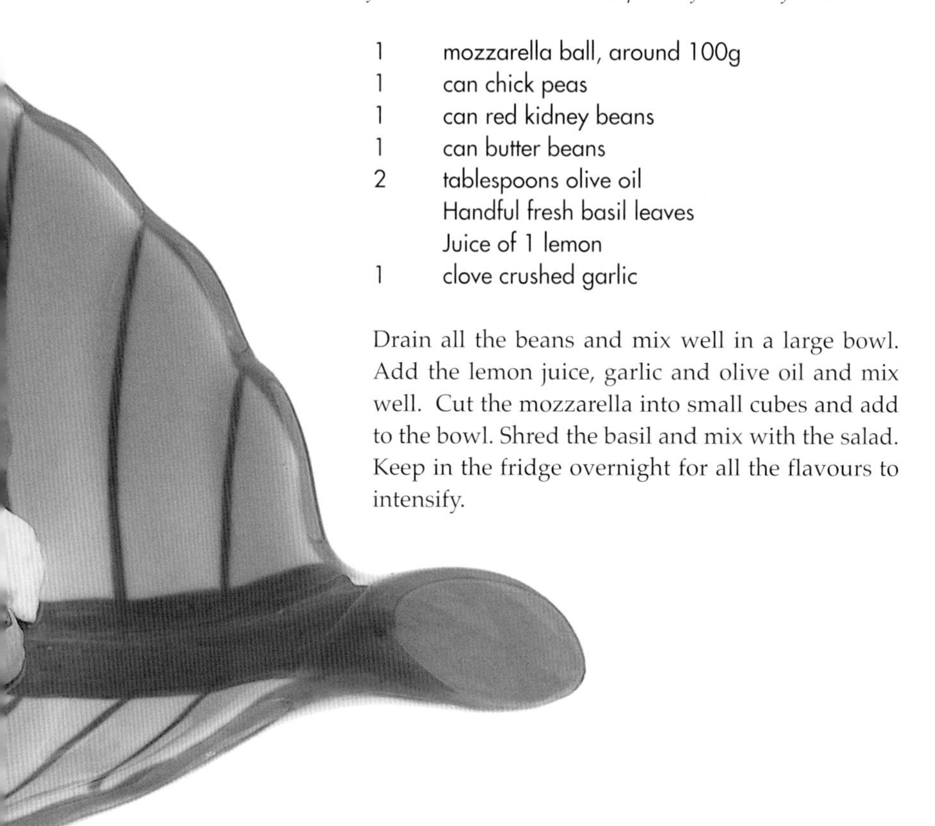

Seafood Salad

Preparation time: 18-20 minutes
Serves 4

350g (12 oz.) mussels
350g (12 oz.) prawns
350g (12 oz.) squid
350g (12 oz.) small scallops
3 lemons
2 tablespoons olive oil
1 red chilli finely chopped
2 cloves crushed garlic
Handful fresh coriander
6 spring onions

In a pan of boiling water add the mussels and prawns and cook until the mussels are fully open. Drain and place to one side. Peel the prawns. Leave the mussels in their shells.

Slice the squid into rings and steam with the scallops over a pan of boiling water in a colander or steamer for 3-5 minutes. Zest the lemons (finely grate the lemon skins) and place in a large bowl. Add the juice of the lemons along with the garlic, chilli and olive oil. Add all the seafood and mix well. Slice the spring onions, roughly chop the coriander and mix with the seafood.

This is at its best if prepared a day in advance as the seafood will really take on the flavours.

Papaya and Squid Salad

Preparation & cooking time: 12 minutes
Serves 4

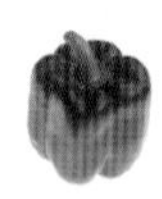

I have never been a fan of fish and fruit but that was before I discovered Thailand. The Thais bring both together with such finesse and delicacy that I have been inspired. Squid has virtually no fat and the papaya has none. So try this for a light, tasty virtually fat free dish

900g	(2 lbs.) squid tubes (cleaned)
2	ripe papayas
1	clove garlic
2	lemongrass stalks
1	teaspoon sugar
4cm	(1½ in.) piece fresh ginger, grated
12	small red chillies
1	teaspoon soy sauce
1	teaspoon fish sauce
1	lime
4	spring onions
	Large handful coriander leaves

To start this dish, slice the squid tubes finely and add to a large heated wok or pan with just a drizzle of oil. Squid cooks quickly so after 2-3 minutes remove from the pan and set aside.

Into a large bowl place the papayas chopped into small cubes. Add the soy sauce, freshly squeezed lime juice, sugar, grated ginger and the fish sauce. Crush the clove of garlic and add to the bowl. Peel the lemongrass stalks until you get to the tender soft part. Chop finely and sprinkle into the bowl along with the chillies also chopped very finely. Slice the spring onions and chopped coriander leaves and add to the bowl along with the squid. Mix well and serve.

Thai Squid Salad

Preparation & cooking time: 10-12 minutes
Serves 4

This is a traditional Thai squid salad. The way I have adapted it to a healthy option with no loss of taste, is eliminating the oil. The only problem you may have is the squid sticking to the pan if not using a non stick wok. In this case, just have a little fish stock or water on hand to add to the pan.

450g (1 lb.) squid
3 stalks lemongrass
4 large lettuce leaves, chopped
1 large tomato cut into 8 wedges
2 tablespoons fish sauce
2 tablespoons lime juice
1 or 2 teaspoons Thai chilli paste or chilli paste or hot pepper sauce
2 teaspoons sugar
2 cloves garlic, minced
2 red chillies, chopped
1 onion, thinly sliced
1 cup fresh mint leaves

Lightly score the squid in a crosshatch pattern using a sharp knife. Do not cut all the way through. Cut ⅔ off each lemongrass stalk and remove roots and outside leaves. Thinly slice the core on the diagonal. Place lettuce leaves on platter or salad plates and arrange tomato wedges on top.

Prepare dressing by whisking together until smooth, fish sauce, lime juice, chilli paste and sugar.

Just before serving, heat wok over a high flame. Add a drizzle of oil followed by garlic, chillies and lemongrass. Stir fry 20 seconds or until fragrant. Add the squid and onions and stir fry until the squid is firm and opaque, about 1 minute. Stir in ½ cup mint leaves. Spoon squid mixture over tomatoes and lettuce leaves. Top with remaining mint leaves and dressing. Serve at once.

Thai Beef Salad (Spicy)

Preparation time: 25 minutes
Serves 4

I love having this dish in Thailand and even I, who can eat the spiciest of foods, have had trouble with it. If you want to make this very spicy then have plenty of rice on hand as rice is the only thing to take the heat out of your mouth. I simplified this dish so it's a really quick recipe.

400g (14 oz.) very lean beef
1 teaspoon olive oil
Salt and pepper
1 teaspoon fish sauce
2 onions
1 bunch fresh coriander
3 tablespoons lemon juice
3 tablespoons fish sauce
1 tablespoon sugar
2-3 chillies

Season the beef with salt, pepper and fish sauce. Fry in a pan with a little oil. Take the beef out of the pan, let it cool then slice.

Slice the onions finely then chop the coriander. Fry onions in a non stick pan with no oil on a low heat.

Mix a sauce with fried onions, coriander, lemon juice, fish sauce and sugar.

Combine beef and sauce and mix. This can be left in the fridge to intensify the flavours.

Thai Spinach

Preparation & cooking time: 10 minutes
Serves 4-6

Although this is called Thai spinach I think it resembles Chinese spinach. Traditionally it is cooked in loads of oil but I have supplemented this with stock. It makes a perfect side dish with fish or meat.

1 tablespoon vegetable oil
4 tablespoons vegetable stock
4 garlic cloves, crushed
4 tablespoons yellow soybean paste
1 red pepper
2 tomatoes, cut into wedges
2 red chillies, sliced
900g (2 lb.) spinach, chopped

Heat the oil in a wok and stir fry the garlic, soybean paste, pepper, tomatoes and chillies for 1 minute. Add the spinach and stock and cook for 3 minutes, stirring frequently. Serve hot and do not overcook.

The Benihana Salad

Preparation time: 8 minutes
Serves 4

This uses the best salad dressing I have ever tasted. I did not need to adapt it much as there is little oil used in the original recipe.

Mixed salad leaves

Dressing

1 small onion
1 celery stick
2.5cm (1 in.) piece ginger
1 medium tomato
3 tablespoons white wine vinegar
1 tablespoon sesame oil
2-3 tablespoons sunflower oil

Place in a blender until smooth. Then dress your salad.

Yoghurt Dressing

Preparation time: 5 minutes
Serves 4-6

150g	(5 oz.) plain yoghurt
1	teaspoon crushed garlic or 1 crushed garlic clove
	Salt
	Pepper
1	heaped teaspoon mustard (dijon is best)
2	spring onions, sliced
2.5cm	(1 in.) piece ginger, grated
	Juice of 1 lemon

Mix well and dress the salad.

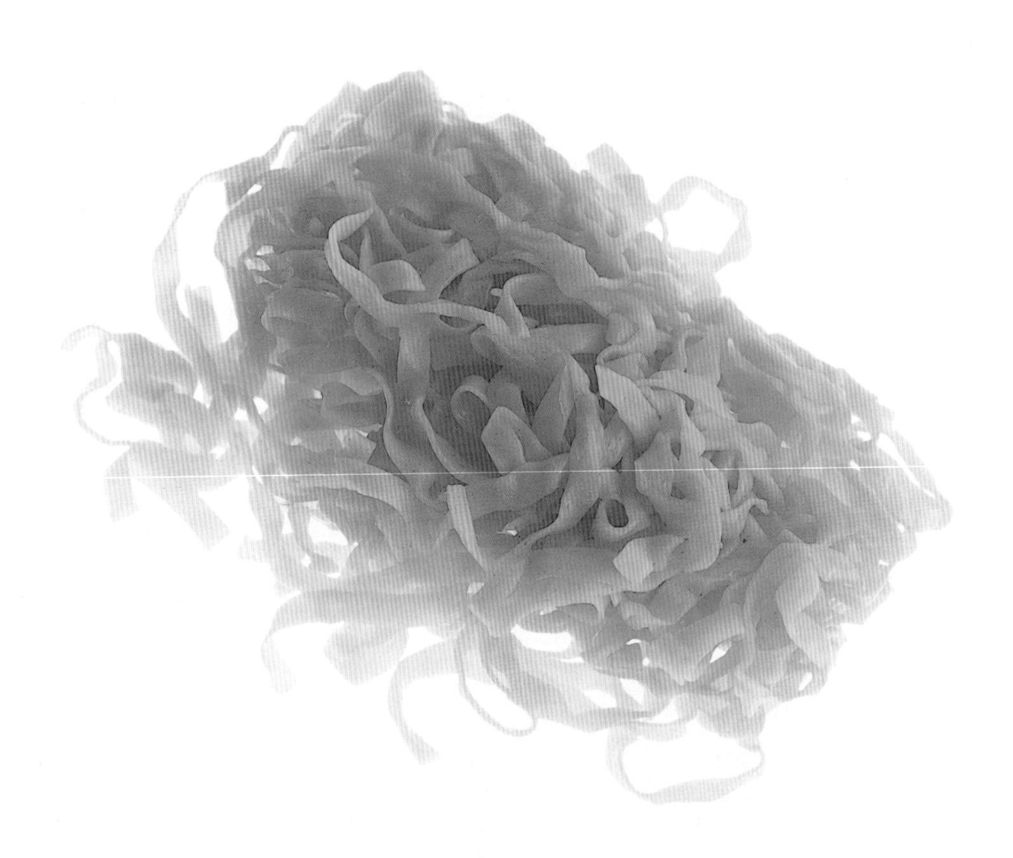

RICE, PASTAS AND NOODLES

Low Fat Pad Thai

Naples in Bangkok

Seafood Risotto

Malaysian Risotto

Healthy Paella

Low Fat Singapore Noodles

Rice Noodles with Prawns

Thai Glass Noodles with Shrimp

Japanese Noodles with Seared Tuna and Teriyaki Sauce

Mozzarella Pizza

Low Fat Pad Thai

Preparation & cooking time: 25 minutes
Serves 2-4

Pad Thai is one of my favourite Thai dishes. I have adapted the traditional method to a healthy low fat version. Thai food has become so popular over the past few years. As long as you ease up on the oil and try not to use the coconut milk it can be very healthy.

1	tablespoon lemon juice
1	teaspoon soy sauce
225g	(½ lb.) bean curd
2	cloves crushed garlic
300g	(10 oz.) dried rice noodles
3	tablespoons brown sugar
3	tablespoons fish sauce
3	eggs
450g	(1 lb.) bean sprouts
4	spring onions
	Coriander leaves to garnish

Start by soaking the rice noodles in boiling water for 5 minutes then drain and leave to one side.

Next, cook the bean curd. Chop it into 1 inch cubes. Take a large non stick wok or frying pan and heat. The best way to stir fry with the least amount of fat is to use a spray of olive oil just coating the pan. Another idea is to drizzle olive oil in the pan then wipe off with a paper towel. This does the same job of lining the pan with oil.

Fry the bean curd for just a minute then add the lemon juice and soy sauce and fry for another minute. Place in a bowl to the side.

Mix the eggs and add to the pan. Break up the eggs in the pan with a wooden spoon then after a minute add the noodles and keep mixing well as you add the sugar, followed by the fish sauce, garlic, bean curd and the bean sprouts. Mix really well and take off the heat.

Slice the spring onions and add to the pan. Place the Pad Thai in a large serving bowl and garnish with chopped coriander.

Bean curd is high in protein and is used often in the vegetarian diet as a replacement for meat, fish and poultry. Many people are put off using it as it has little flavour. If you experiment with it you can get some great results. The way I have fried this with lemon and soy gives a caramelised texture and taste and really works well.

Naples in Bangkok

Preparation & cooking time: 20 minutes
Serves: 4

This is what I call fusion food, where you take the wonderful flavours of Italy and throw in some Thai herbs and spices. I like this dish very spicy but add chillies to your taste.

A tip for all pastas. When you make a sauce always add the pasta to the pan your sauce is in and cook for a minute. This allows the flavours to cook into the pasta.

450g (1 lb.) spaghetti
Water for boiling
1 onion, chopped
1 clove garlic, minced
2 tablespoons tomato paste
650g (1½ lbs.) cherry tomatoes, halved
2-3 small red chillies, chopped finely
2.5cm (1 in.) piece grated ginger
2 lemongrass stalks peeled and finely chopped
Handful fresh coriander leaves

Cook pasta in a large pot of boiling water according to instructions. Drain and rinse with cold water.

While the pasta is cooking, heat a pan with a drizzle of olive oil and add the onion. Fry for a minute then add the garlic, tomatoes and tomato paste. Cook on a gentle heat for 5 minutes. So far this is just a traditional tomato sauce but now we make it with a Thai twist.

Add to the pan the lemongrass, ginger and chillies. Cover and cook for another 8-10 minutes then add the pasta to the pan. Remove from heat and add the coriander, roughly chopped. It is now ready to serve.

Seafood Risotto

Preparation & cooking time: 35-40 minutes
Serves 4

300g (11 oz.) risotto rice
1 litre (1¾ pints) of stock (fish or vegetable)
1 large onion
2 large carrots
1 glass white wine (optional)
2 cloves garlic
225g (½ lb.) peeled prawns
225g (½ lb.) squid tubes
450g (1 lb.) fresh tuna
450g (1 lb.) queen scallops
Olive oil for frying
Handful fresh basil leaves rolled up and sliced

Finely chop the onion and carrots. In a pan bring the stock to simmering point and turn the heat to low. In a large frying pan heat a little olive oil and fry the onion and carrots but do not brown. Add the risotto rice and fry for about 1 minute turning the ingredients to prevent sticking. Add the wine and hear the pan sizzle. If you are not using the wine use a ladle of stock. Once this has been absorbed add a ladle at a time without ever drowning the rice in liquid. Keep adding a ladle at a time during the next 20-25 minutes depending on whether you like your risotto al dente or not. If you have any remaining stock discard it.

Five minutes before the risotto is ready cut the squid tubes into rings and add to the risotto followed by the tuna which should be cut into cubes. Then add the scallops. Cooking the seafood should only take a few minutes. Turn off the heat, add the prawns, stir in the fresh basil and season.

Malaysian Risotto

Preparation & cooking time: 30 minutes
Serves 4

300g	(11 oz.) risotto rice
1	litre (1¾ pints) of stock (fish or vegetable)
1	large onion
2	garlic cloves, crushed
900g	(2 lb.) chicken
2	lemongrass stalks
1	teaspoon grated fresh ginger
1	red chilli
2	lime leaves
	Sesame oil for frying
	Handful fresh coriander leaves

Chop finely the onion. In a pan, bring the stock to simmering point and turn the heat down low. In a large saucepan, heat a little sesame oil and fry the onion but do not brown. Then add the risotto rice. Try to wait as long as possible (about 1 minute) before adding the stock. Keep the rice moving to prevent sticking. Add a ladle of stock followed by the chilli finely chopped, grated ginger, crushed garlic and the lime leaves. Dice the chicken and add to the pan. Once the stock has been absorbed, add a ladle at a time for 20-25 minutes without drowning the rice in liquid. If you like your risotto al dente, add less stock. Discard the lime leaves and add the coriander roughly chopped. Your risotto is now ready to serve.

Healthy Paella

Preparation & cooking time: 40-45 minutes
Serves 6-8

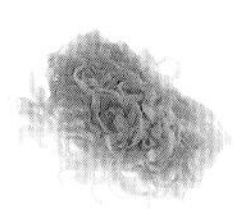

10	chicken pieces (the legs, thighs, wings and breasts)
2	garlic cloves, crushed
350g	(12 oz.) squid
350g	(12 oz.) prawns
18	mussels
4	rashers bacon (optional)
1	large red pepper
3	onions
1	cup chicken stock
6	large tomatoes, peeled and chopped
1	tablespoon olive oil
350g	(12 oz.) long grain rice
	Few strands on saffron
	Lemon wedges to serve

I love this classic Spanish dish but I have adapted it using bacon as the traditional chorizo (pepperoni) although lovely, is very high in fat.

In a very large pan add olive oil and fry the chicken pieces until brown. Remove and put aside. Chop the onions finely and add to the same pan cooking on a low heat for a few minutes. Add garlic and rice and coat in the oil. Return the chicken pieces to the pan and mix well. Remove all the fat from the bacon, chop the lean meat and add to the pan. Now you can add the stock followed by the tomatoes and red pepper that should also be cut finely.

Cover with a lid and cook on a low heat for 20 minutes. Then add the saffron and more stock if needed and cook again covered for another 15 minutes.

Now add the seafood. The squid should be in rings, the mussels cleaned and the prawns left with their shells on. Mix well and cook until the prawns have turned pink and the mussels are fully open.

Serve with large wedges of lemon.

Low Fat Singapore Noodles

Preparation & cooking time: 50 minutes
Serves 8

I love Singapore noodles and whenever I am in Asia I always take it for breakfast from the buffet. The problem is they are normally cooked with a lot of oil so I have adapted yet again. Use soba noodles as they are easy to find.

- 400g (14 oz.) soba noodles
- ½ cup dried shrimp
- 1 egg
- 1 tablespoon water
- 225g (8 oz.) barbecued pork (fat removed)
- 2 stalks celery
- 2 cups bean sprouts, blanched
- 1 medium yellow onion
- 1 green pepper (capsicum)
- 1 medium firm tomato
- 2 cloves garlic, minced
- 1 teaspoon fresh ginger, minced
- 1 tablespoon curry powder
- 1 teaspoon sesame oil

Sauce

- ½ cup stock
- 2 teaspoons soy sauce
- 1 teaspoon sugar

Bring a pan of water to the boil and add noodles just to heat through. Drain, reserving boiling water, and rinse with cold water until noodles are cooled and will not stick together. Place in an oiled bowl and refrigerate until firm. The noodles must be firm before frying and can be prepared a day before.

Wash then soak the dried shrimp for 30 minutes. Cut into thin pieces. Combine egg and water and cook as a very thin omelette. Cool and slice into 5cm (2 in.) long shreds. Thinly slice the pork to match.

Blanch bean sprouts in noodle water. Peel strings off celery stalks before slicing thinly. Peel and halve onions then slice thinly. Core the pepper and slice thinly into 5cm (2 in.) lengths. Slice the tomato into thin wedges. An alternative is to slice all the vegetables to match the size of the bean sprouts for a better looking dish (a good shredder does this job quickly).

Mix sauce ingredients in a bowl. Heat 1 teaspoon sesame oil in a wok. When oil begins to smoke, toss in garlic, ginger, dried shrimp and vegetables except the tomato. Stir fry on a high heat for two minutes. Add the sauce and continue cooking until the sauce reduces by half. Remove to a bowl.

Rinse the wok and return it to high heat. When it is dry, reduce the heat to medium and add 1 teaspoon sesame oil but don't let it smoke. Add curry powder, stirring to mix with oil. Avoid burning curry. If it burns, start over. Cook curry powder for about 30 seconds. Add noodles a fistful at a time, breaking the noodles into short pieces. Toss noodles to coat and heat them. When hot, add cooked shrimp and vegetables. Toss together to mix. Turn off the heat. Add pork, egg shreds and tomato wedges. Mix together. Serve. By the time this dish is on the table, tomatoes will be hot, but still firm.

Rice Noodles with Prawns

Preparation & cooking time: 30 minutes
Serves 4

I have only recently started using rice noodles. The beauty of them is they are fat free and as they are made from rice they are complex carbohydrates. These are the best carbohydrates for your body. So if you are on those silly protein only diets, you are missing out.

300g (11 oz.) rice noodles
300g (11 oz.) prawns
1 tablespoon olive oil or sesame oil
1 tablespoon soy sauce
500g (18 oz.) broccoli
2 eggs, beaten
3 tablespoons fish sauce
3 tablespoons sweet soy sauce
1 tablespoon sugar

In a large pot bring water to the boil and cook the rice noodles for five minutes. Drain and rinse with cold water.

Cut the broccoli into bite size pieces and boil in lightly salted water. Remove from water, rinse in cold water and set aside. If you rinse any green vegetables in cold water after cooking, it preserves their colour.

Wash the prawns then heat the oil in a wok or a pan. Add the prawns and stir fry. Push prawns to one side and quickly add beaten eggs. Once they begin to set, gently scramble them. Stir prawns and eggs. Add broccoli and stir fry.

Add noodles, fish sauce, soy sauce and sugar and stir well. Now it's ready to serve and enjoy.

Thai Glass Noodles with Shrimp

Preparation & cooking time: 12 minutes
Serves 4-6

I love this simple version of Thai noodles which can work very well with a large salad.

Glass noodles are very low in fat and all I have done is eliminate the oil altogether to make it fat free.

250g (9 oz.) glass noodles
450g (1 lb.) peeled cooked small shrimp
1 tablespoon soy sauce
1 tablespoon fish sauce
2 lemongrass stalks, peeled and finely chopped
1 clove crushed garlic
2 small red chillies chopped finely
2.5cm (1 in.) ginger grated
Handful fresh coriander leaves roughly chopped

Place the glass noodles in a bowl and cover with boiling water for 5-8 minutes, drain and place to one side.

In a wok add the noodles followed by all the above ingredients and fry for just a few minutes. Serve in a large bowl.

Japanese Noodles with Seared Tuna and Teriyaki Sauce

Preparation & cooking time: 25 minutes
Serves 4

1 pack of large egg noodles
4 spring onions (chopped)
1 teaspoon sesame oil
1 teaspoon soy sauce
1 tuna steak
2 tablespoons sesame seeds

Teriyaki Glaze
3 tablespoons soy sauce
6 tablespoons dry sherry
1 tablespoon sugar
2 teaspoons honey
3 tablespoons water

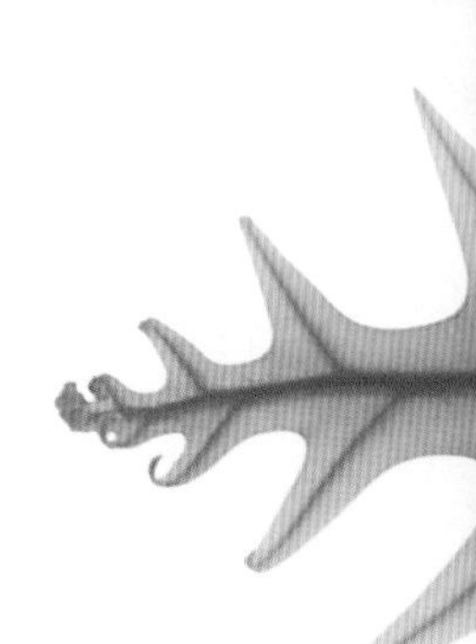

Begin by making the teriyaki glaze by putting all the ingredients in a pan over a medium heat and reducing them until you have a thick sauce. Pour the sauce into a bowl.

Take a wok and a frying pan and in the wok heat the sesame oil and add the noodles. Fry for just a couple of minutes then add the spring onions and soy sauce and remove from the heat. Heat the frying pan with a little oil. Coat the tuna steak with sesame seeds and sear in the pan on a high heat for 1-2 minutes each side. Remove and place on a cutting board.

To serve, place a small pile of noodles on a plate, slice the tuna and put 3-4 pieces on top of the noodles.

Drizzle the teriyaki glaze around the plate and serve.

Mozzarella Pizza

Preparation & cooking time: 25 minutes
Serves 4

I love pizza and you don't always need cheese to make it fantastic. The original pizza was just dough, tomatoes, garlic and basil. If you do use cheese, use fresh mozzarella: there is such a difference.

1	mozzarella ball, around 100g
1	ready made pizza dough
4	tablespoons tomato puree
1	can tomatoes blended
2	cloves crushed garlic
	Handful fresh basil leaves
	Handful olives

Blend the canned tomatoes in a blender until smooth and place in a large bowl together with the tomato puree and garlic. Mix well.

Spread the tomato mixture on the pizza dough. Slice the mozzarella and place evenly on the pizza. Dot it with some olives, sprinkle shredded basil. Place in an oven for 15-20 minutes (read the pizza package for oven temperature and cooking time) and serve with a salad.

FISH & SEAFOOD

Fresh Tuna on Spicy Salsa

Lemon Tuna

Asian Spice Tuna on Wasabi Carrot Mash

Salmon Fish Cakes

Everything Salmon

Salmon in Cous Cous over Wasabi Mashed Potato and Avocado Salsa

Paupiettes of Sea Bass

Sea Bass with Thai Spice

Grilled Snow Fish on Asian Rice

Red Snapper Steamed with Chilli

Lobster with Ginger Sauce

Tiger Prawns on Mango Salsa

Stuffed Squid in Red Sauce

Stuffed Squid

Fresh Tuna on Spicy Salsa

Preparation & cooking time: 8-12 minutes
Serves 4

I like to cook this rare but only if it is bought on the same day as it is eaten. Some people like fresh tuna cooked all the way through but I feel you may as well used tinned if this is the case.

4	tuna steaks
1	tablespoon olive oil
	Bunch fresh coriander leaves
8	medium tomatoes deseeded
1	red onion
½	red chilli
1	clove crushed garlic
	Juice of 1 lime or 1 lemon

To make the salsa, chop the onion, tomatoes and coriander very finely and place in a bowl. Add to this the garlic and lime juice. Cut the chilli finely, remove the seeds if you don't like it hot, and add to the bowl.

In a large frying pan heat a little oil and sear the tuna. This will take one minute each side for rare. If you do not like your tuna rare you can press down on the steak in the pan: if it is not soft it will be cooked through.

Arrange a large spoonful of salsa on a plate then place the tuna steak on top and serve.

Lemon Tuna

Preparation & cooking time: 8-10 minutes
Serves 4

4	large tuna steaks
3	lemons
2	tablespoons olive oil
	Handful fresh chives or green tips of spring onions

This reminds me of Italy. So simple and so fresh and wonderful in flavour.

In a frying pan add a drop of oil and fry the tuna steaks 2-4 minutes each side depending on how you like your tuna. I think it's best on the rare side.

Meanwhile grate your lemons with a zester and when finished, squeeze all the juice into a bowl. Cut the chives or green spring onion leaf tips and place in a bowl. When you have turned the tuna steaks over add the lemon juice, the zest and the oil. Just as you turn off the heat throw in the chives and coat well.

This is perfect on a summer's day served with a salad.

Asian Spice Tuna on Wasabi Carrot Mash

Preparation & cooking time: 40 minutes
Serves 4

4 tuna steaks
12 large carrots
150ml (5 fl.oz.) semi or skimmed milk
2-4 teaspoons wasabi paste
Juice of 4 limes
2 tablespoons soy sauce
1½ tablespoons sesame oil
4 tablespoons finely chopped shallots
2 red chillies (deseeded optional) and finely chopped
2 teaspoons fresh grated ginger
2 lemongrass stalks, finely chopped
8 spring onions
3-4 cloves crushed garlic
1 tablespoon olive oil
Large handful of fresh coriander

Start by making the wasabi carrot mash which can be prepared ahead of time. Peel and halve the carrots and place in a saucepan of boiling water for about 25 minutes. They are ready when a knife glides easily through them. Using an electric or hand whisk, start to puree the carrots slowly adding the milk and wasabi paste. Add 2 teaspoons of wasabe paste for a hint and four for a kick. Put to one side. You can reheat this later.

In a non stick frying pan add a little olive oil and fry the spring onions for a few minutes until they brown slightly. Remove and set aside. In the same pan fry the tuna steaks. For the best result, cook for 1 minute each side or longer if you do not like them rare in the middle. You will probably find it easiest to cook two at a time. Just when they are ready, remove them and add to the frying pan the olive oil and shallots, then the garlic. Fry for 30 seconds then add the chilli and ginger, sesame oil, soy sauce, lime juice and lemongrass. Before you chop the lemongrass, peel off and discard the outer tougher layers and use the softer more tender part of the stalk. Quickly add the tuna steaks and coat in the spices.

On a plate, make a ring of carrot wasabi mash then place a spring onion on each side of the plate. Put the tuna steak in the middle and drizzle a little sauce over it if there is any left in the pan. Garnish with chopped coriander and serve.

Salmon Fish Cakes

Preparation & cooking time: 15-20 minutes
Serves 4

Salmon is a fish that is high in natural fats but low in saturated fat. If you are not having much fat in your diet, this is an ideal way to get the right sort of fats the body needs. I suggest you add 2 chillies as it needs a kick and the heat works well.

450g	(1 lb.) fresh salmon fillets
1	egg
1-2	red chillies (seeds retained depending how hot you want)
4	spring onions
	Juice of half a lemon
	Handful fresh coriander leaves
2	lemongrass stalks, peeled
1	teaspoon fresh ginger
1	teaspoon soy sauce
1	teaspoon fish sauce (optional)
2	tablespoons olive oil

In a blender whiz the salmon, red chilli, lemon juice, egg, lemongrass, ginger, fish sauce and soy sauce. Then slice the spring onions, chop the coriander and mix into the salmon mixture. You can make this ahead of time and leave in the fridge.

When you are ready to serve, heat a large frying pan and make your salmon mixture into balls. Add a drizzle of olive oil or better than that, spray the pan with an oil can spray. Add the fish cakes three at a time to the pan and cook for 2-3 minutes each side. As there is little fat in the mixture and no bread to bind it, you must not move the cakes around the pan until they are ready to turn or they will crumble.

As we are cutting out carbohydrate and fat in this dish I strongly recommend salmon.

Everything Salmon

Preparation & cooking time 20 minutes
Serves 4

A spectacular looking starter that would make any dinner party look impressive. All can be made ahead of time with ease.

3	salmon fillets
1	jar salmon eggs
1	small avocado
2	cups low fat yoghurt
½	red onion
	Juice of 1 lemon
1	bay leaf
	Peppercorns

This dish consists of three separate items. A salmon paté (fat free); a portion of poached salmon; and lastly, salmon tartare with salmon eggs over a layer of avocado.

Take two of the salmon fillets and remove two inches from each end. Set aside for later. Cut each remaining piece into two. Place these four fillets in a large saucepan, cover with water just to the top of the salmon and throw in a bay leaf and some peppercorns. Bring to the boil, remove from the heat, cover and leave to stand for six minutes. When time is up, remove the poached salmon.

Next you can make the salmon paté. In a blender place half a salmon fillet, the yoghurt, lemon juice and seasoning to taste. Blend to a paste then quarter fill four ramekins. Cover with foil and boil in a saucepan with water reaching half way up the side of the ramekins. Cover the pot and simmer for 8 minutes on a low heat. Remove each mousse from its ramekin when cool.

Lastly there is the salmon tartare. Slice and chop as finely as possible all the remaining salmon. Do the same with the onion and mix together. In small rings (moulds) placed on the serving plate, quarter fill with finely chopped avocado and a little lemon juice to stop it browning, then add the raw salmon mixture and top with a thin layer of salmon eggs. Remove the ring and you will be left with a perfect round salmon tartare.

Arrange one piece of poached salmon and a portion of the smoked salmon paté neatly on the same plate. Repeat this on each plate and there you have it.

Salmon in Cous Cous over Wasabi Mashed Potato and Avocado Salsa

Preparation & cooking time: 40 minutes
Serves 4

I think I have used this recipe on everyone I know because it is just so simple to prepare everything ahead of time.

4 salmon fillets, skinned
200g (7 oz.) cous cous
1 egg

Mashed Potato
4-5 potatoes
5 tablespoons milk
Spring onions
1-2 teaspoons wasabi paste

Avocado Salsa
1 avocado
4 large tomatoes, deseeded and chopped
2 tablespoons fresh coriander
Spring onions
Juice of 1 lime or half a lemon
Salt and pepper

The salmon can be prepared ahead of time by placing it in the refrigerator earlier the same day.

Whisk an egg in a bowl and set aside. Put the cous cous in a large bowl and cover to just above the surface with boiling water. Cover with a plate and leave for 5 minutes. When ready fluff up the cous cous with a fork.

Dip the salmon fillets in the egg then into the cous cous bowl. Use your hands to coat the entire piece of salmon with the cous cous. Place the salmon on a baking tray and leave in the fridge until you are ready to cook.

For the mash, peel the potatoes and quarter. Boil them for 20-25 minutes. When ready, either pop through a potato ricer or drain the water then with the lid on, shake vigorously to break up the potatoes. Add the wasabi paste then mash with a fork or masher until smooth. Add chopped spring onions to the potatoes together with milk and salt. Mix well. I usually prepare this in the morning, leave in the

refrigerator and warm up in the microwave.

For the salsa, chop the spring onions and place in a bowl, adding the lime juice. The chopped tomatoes, roughly shredded coriander and the avocado cut into small cubes can be mixed in. Set aside.

The salmon will need to cook in a fan assisted oven at 180° (200° regular) or gas mark 6 for 18-20 minutes. When ready, place the warm mashed potatoes in a pastry ring, pushing down hard so when you lift it up, it leaves a perfect circle of mash. Place a piece of salmon on top and make 3 small spoonfuls of salsa around the edges.

If you do not have a pastry ring you can cut out both ends of a plastic lined can and use that. I still have one that I re-use as it's a perfect size.

Paupiettes of Sea Bass

Preparation & cooking time: 40-45 minutes
Serves 4

This has to be my favourite recipe as it has all the flavours of Asia and is such a fresh meal. It is also fantastic with monkfish. When you cut open the foil the whole room is filled with aromatic smells that just make you want to tuck in. With supermarkets stocking ingredients such as lemongrass and pak choi you really can bring the world to your table without the fuss of having to go to speciality shops.

4 thick fillets of sea bass
4 spring onions
2 leeks
200ml (7 fl.oz.) dry white wine
4 lemongrass stalks
Juice of 1 lemon
1 large carrot
4 large mushrooms
12 new potatoes
2 tablespoons cream
1 small red chilli

For four servings, take four large squares of silver foil. Make each piece into the shape of a large bowl. Now double it up with another sheet of foil so that you have four bowls each with two layers. Set aside.

Cut the leeks in half then shred them lengthways as finely as possible. Split the shredded leeks into four portions and place each portion at the bottom of each foil parcel. Next add a spring onion to each followed by a lemongrass stalk which should be cut in half. Now add 3 new potatoes halved again to each parcel. Cut the mushrooms in half and also divide to each parcel. Deseed the red chilli, chop finely and add a little to each parcel. Peel the carrot then shred finely and place on top of the leeks. You can now add on top of the leeks the fillets of sea bass.

In a bowl mix the white wine, cream and lemon juice and season well. Divide the liquid into four and pour over the sea bass.

Take four more large squares of silver foil and cover each parcel making a dome. Fold the joins well so it is airtight.

Place the parcels in a pre-heated fan assisted oven at 160°C (180°C regular) or gas mark 4 for 35-40 minutes. When ready, place each parcel on a plate and take to the table. Once you have served your guests at the table, make an incision in each parcel all the way through the top. This dish is eaten in the foil which retains all the flavours and aromas right in front of you.

Sea Bass with Thai Spice

Preparation & cooking time: 35-40 minutes
Serves 1

I make this dish all the time for myself. It is so low in fat and very high in flavour. I get such compliments when serving it but dinner guests do not realise how easy it is. Remember, look the fish in the eye. If it is cloudy it is not fresh.

1	whole sea bass
1	lemon
1	tablespoon fish sauce
1	clove garlic
2.5cm	(1 in.) piece ginger
	Handful fresh coriander
1	small red chilli

Gash the sea bass 3 or 4 times on each side to make small cavities. Place on a large sheet of tin foil and set aside.

On a large chopping board using a mezzaluna or a knife, chop finely the garlic, coriander, ginger and chilli. Place a little of the mixture in each cavity you cut in the fish. If you have any left over, place in the gutted part of the fish.

Squeeze the lemon over the fish along with the fish sauce, seal the foil and place in a fan assisted oven at 200°C (220°C regular oven) or gas mark 6, for 30 minutes.

Unseal and eat from the foil if you like.

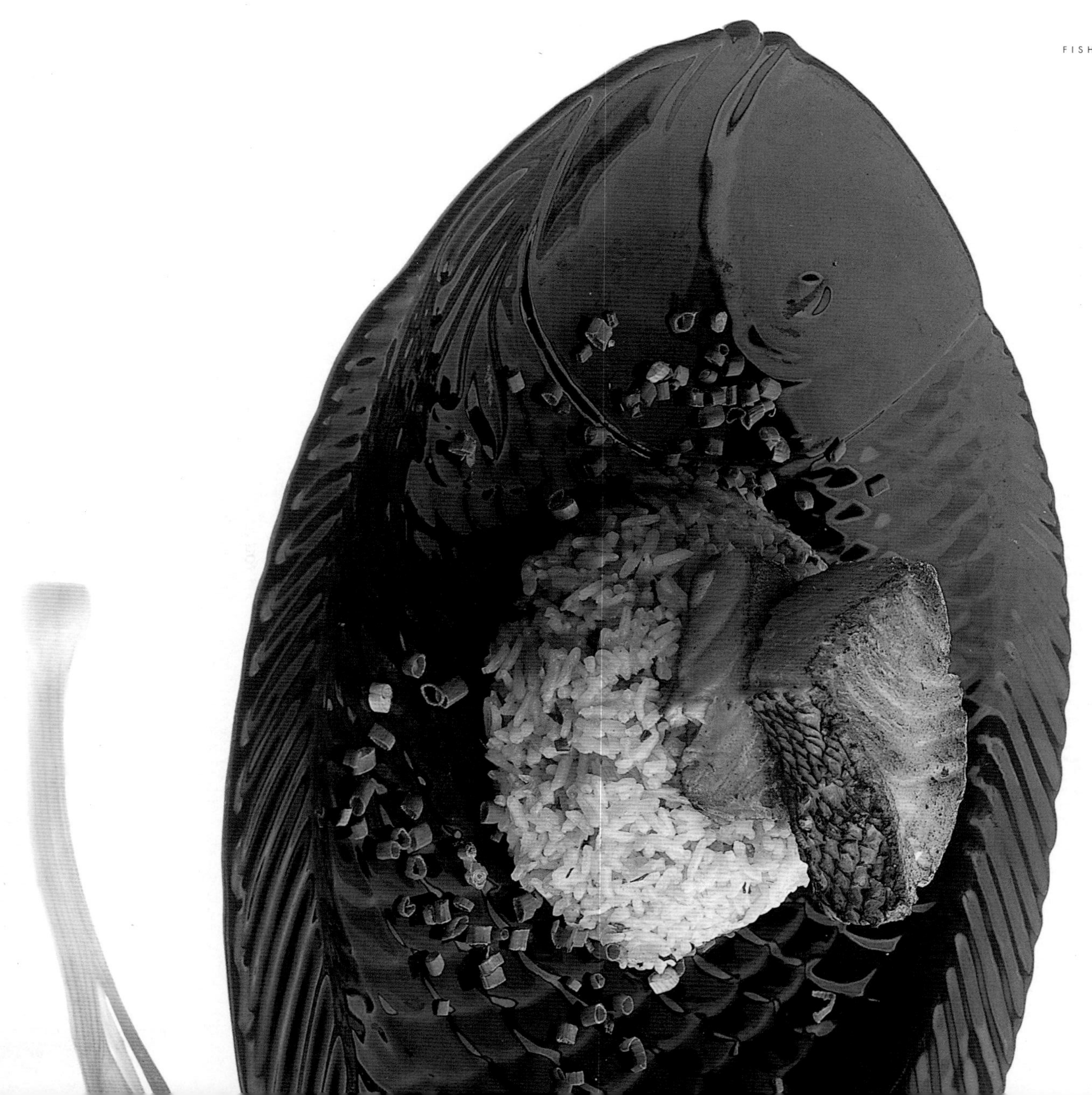

Grilled Snow Fish on Asian Rice

Preparation & cooking time: 25 minutes
Serves 4

4 snow fish fillets
600ml (1 pint) vegetable stock or water
2 lemongrass stalks
1 teaspoon freshly grated ginger
2 garlic cloves crushed
6 spring onions
1 small onion
1 small red chilli
300g (11 oz.) rice (any rice will do but long grain is perfect)
Handful fresh coriander leaves

This is a great dish for subtle flavours. It brings out all these spices and herbs but in a very smooth way.

Chop the onion finely and fry in a large saucepan with a little olive oil. Add the rice and coat with the hot oil. Add stock or water and garlic, chilli, ginger and finely chopped lemongrass. (Use only the inner part of the lemongrass.) Place a lid over the pan and simmer for 20 minutes. Add more liquid if you feel it needs any.

In a frying pan with ridges, cook the snow fish 3-4 minutes each side. If you do not have a barbecue style pan, place in the oven under the grill for the same time.

Slice the spring onions and add to the rice. Mix well.

Serve the rice on a plate followed by the snow fish and a garnish of coriander leaves.

Red Snapper Steamed with Chilli

Preparation & cooking time: 18 minutes
Serves 4

I love steamed fish. You can't get a healthier meal. But steamed fish can be bland so this recipe packs a punch with aromatic spices. Your kitchen will remind you of Thailand as you cook this meal.

4 red snapper fillets
3 small red chillies
2.5cm (1 in.) piece ginger
1 tablespoon soy sauce
1 tablespoon fish sauce
2 teaspoons sesame oil
2 lemongrass stalks
4 lime leaves
2 teaspoons sesame seeds

Place the snapper fillets in a bowl and add the marinade of soy sauce, sesame oil, fish sauce, grated ginger, chopped chillies (with or without seeds) and finely chopped lemongrass. Chill for at least an hour.

In a large steamer, place each fillet on top of a lime leaf. Spoon the marinade on top of the fillets. Sprinkle with sesame seeds and steam over boiling water for 10-12 minutes. Serve with salad or rice.

Lobster with Ginger Sauce

Preparation & cooking time: 25 minutes
Serves 4

2 lobsters

Sauce

2 tablespoons soy sauce
1 clove garlic, crushed
1 lemongrass stalk, chopped finely
2.5cm (1 in.) piece ginger, grated
1 tablespoon olive oil
1 teaspoon sugar
2 shallots, diced
1 teaspoon lemon juice

Grill the lobster whole for 15 minutes. Remove meat from the shell and insert a wooden skewer into each end to keep the meat in place.

Mix together the sauce ingredients and place in a dish to accompany the lobster.

Tiger Prawns on Mango Salsa

Preparation & cooking time: 25 minutes
Serves 4

12	large tiger prawns
½	large mango
	Fresh coriander (handful)
4	spring onions
1	tablespoon white sesame seeds
1	lime
1	teaspoon soy sauce
1	red chilli
1	clove of garlic
1	teaspoon sesame oil

Start by making the salsa. Chop the mango into small cubes and place in a bowl. Add to this chopped coriander, the crushed clove of garlic, the chopped spring onion and finely chopped chilli, soy sauce, sesame seeds and oil, and the juice of the lime. Mix well.

Leaving the tail on the tiger prawns, remove their shells and devein them. In a large non stick pan drizzle some olive oil and fry the prawns until they turn completely pink .

Arrange the prawns on top of the salsa and serve.

Stuffed Squid in Red Sauce

Preparation & cooking time: 15-18 minutes
Serves 4-6

I love squid and it's fat free. Instead of deep frying in breadcrumbs like we do in Europe, try this alternative. Squid can go like rubber if cooked too long so don't worry about cooking quickly. You will see the difference.

325g	(12 oz.) lean ground pork
½	cup coarsely chopped bamboo shoots
¼	cup coarsely chopped water chestnuts
1	teaspoon ground black pepper
1	teaspoon finely chopped garlic
1	coriander stem with root, finely chopped
½	teaspoon sugar
2	tablespoons fish sauce
1-2	whole squid tubes, cleaned with cavities intact

Sauce

¼	cup canned tomatoes
½	cup dry red wine
¼	cup soy sauce
1	tablespoon sugar
1	teaspoon ground black pepper

In a large bowl mix the pork, bamboo, chestnuts, pepper, garlic, coriander, sugar and fish sauce. Refrigerate for half an hour. Stuff the raw squid with the pork mixture so that they are puffed and cylindrical. Place the stuffed squid on a flat steamer or steam tray and steam for 8-10 minutes or until the squid turns opaque. Remove from heat and set aside while preparing the sauce.

Preheat a fan assisted oven to 210°C (230°C regular oven) gas mark 8. In a saucepan, melt butter over low heat. Add the tomatoes, stirring to blend. Stir in the wine, soy sauce, sugar and pepper. Bring to a boil and add one cup of water. Return to a simmer for 5-7 minutes. While the sauce is simmering, arrange the steamed squid in a single layer in a deep casserole dish. Pour the sauce over the squid and cover. Bake for 30 minutes, serve with steamed rice.

Stuffed Squid

Preparation & cooking time: 25 minutes
Serves 4

This is an Italian classic which adapts itself perfectly to a fat free recipe. You can also use any herbs and spices you like. I have added chilli and lemongrass to give a Thai feel. Squid has no fat but is high in cholesterol.

2 lemongrass stalks
200g (7 oz.) Thai jasmine rice
10-12 squid tubes
4 tomatoes
1 red chilli
1 tin chopped tomatoes
1 clove garlic

Boil the rice for 12 minutes, strain and place in a bowl. To the bowl add the garlic, 4 tomatoes finely chopped and the chilli with seeds finely sliced. Peel away the hard layers of the lemongrass and chop finely the tender stalk. Add to the bowl and mix well.

Line a large baking tray with foil. Stuff the squid tubes with as much of the mixture as will go in and place on the baking tray. Cook in a fan assisted oven at 180°C (200°C regular) or gas mark 6 for 8-12 minutes . While you are doing this, blend until smooth the chopped canned tomatoes, transfer to a pan and heat gently.

To serve, drop a few spoonfuls of tomato sauce on a plate with the squid tubes on top.

If you like spice, add a chilli to the canned tomatoes before blending

Pork, Chicken, Lamb and Beef

Pork Teriyaki and Apple Sauce

Preparation and cooking time: 50 minutes
Serves 4

500g (17 oz.) lean pork
1 apple peeled and cored

Teriyaki Sauce
3 tablespoons soy sauce
6 tablespoons dry sherry
1 tablespoon sugar
2 teaspoons honey
3 tablespoons water

Drizzle the pork with olive oil and roast in a fan assisted oven at 200°C (220°C regular) or gas mark 7 for 30 minutes. Remove from oven and let it rest.

Meanwhile, put all the ingredients for the teriyaki sauce into a pan over a medium heat, reducing them until you have a thick sauce. Chop the apple and add to the sauce. Place the pork in the sauce for a few minutes to absorb the flavours, then serve.

Thai Pork with Cucumber

Preparation & cooking time: 25 minutes
Serves 4

People forget that pork can be a low fat meat. As long as you remove the fat it can be as lean as chicken. It's also inexpensive so try it now and again. What I love about Thai food is however spicy you make it you can still taste the ingredients as Thai spices never overpower.

450g (1 lb.) pork fillets (lean)
2 cloves garlic
2 spring onions
1 cucumber
1 tablespoon olive oil
3 tablespoons fish sauce
3 tablespoons oyster sauce
1 tablespoon sugar
2 eggs, beaten

Slice the meat and chop the garlic. Dice the cucumber and cut the spring onions into 2cm (1 in.) pieces.

Heat oil in a wok or a pan and stir fry garlic until golden. Add the meat and stir fry for 3-4 minutes. Add the cucumber to the pan then the onions, fish sauce, oyster sauce and sugar. Continue to stir fry for two minutes.

Push the meat to one side of the pan and quickly add the beaten eggs. Once they begin to set, gently scramble them. Stir eggs into the meat. Serve.

Pork Stir Fry

Preparation & cooking time: 23 minutes
Serves 4

This is a dish that you can just throw all the ingredients into a pan and not fuss or worry about the cooking. It's healthy, tasty and easy. Pork is not used in the West as much as it is in the East. I am not sure why as it has more flavour than chicken and is as low in fat as long as you use the lean part.

900g (2 lbs.) lean pork
1 teaspoon olive oil
1 teaspoon tomato paste
1 clove garlic (crushed)
2.5cm (1in.) ginger, grated
1 cup stock vegetable or chicken
450g (½ lb.) mixed vegetables
1 teaspoon soy sauce

In a pan heat the oil and fry the pork. As soon as it has browned, add the vegetables then the tomato paste and garlic followed by the soy sauce, ginger and stock. Bring to the boil and simmer for 15 minutes. Serve.

Chinese Chicken in Lettuce Wrap

Preparation & cooking time: 40 minutes
Serves 4-6.

Everyone will love this dish. It's an alternative to Chinese or Peking duck in pancakes and fun for a dinner party. It's also great for people on a low carbohydrate diet. If you are on one of these diets, you run out of ideas fast, so try this one.

Carbohydrate is best eaten in the morning to enable the body to burn it off. If consumed in large quantities it can turn to fat. Try eating less during the evening meal but long term, do not try and go on a carbohydrate free regime. Your body needs carbohydrates.

- 1 lettuce
- 700g (1½ lbs.) lean chicken mince
- ½ can water chestnuts
- 6 large mushrooms (shitake are best)
- ½ large onion
- 1 clove crushed garlic
- 1 tablespoon oyster sauce
- 1 tablespoon soy sauce
- 1 tablespoon sherry
- 2 tablespoons cornflour mixed with a little water
- Plum sauce (optional if you do not want the carbohydrates)

Finely chop the onion, mushrooms and water chestnuts. Mix 2 tablespoons of water with the cornflour in a separate bowl and whisk until smooth. In a large bowl add the chicken mince along with the mushrooms, onion, water chestnuts and garlic. Add the soy sauce and the oyster sauce as well as the cornflour mix and the sherry. Combine together - you will find it easier to use your hands.

On a serving plate separate the lettuce leaves and place on the table. Pour some good quality plum sauce into a small dish and place next to the lettuce. Fry the chicken mixture in a large frying pan or wok for 15-20 minutes. Keep the mixture moving with a wooden spoon as you do not want it to end up as one big burger. When cooked, place in a serving dish. Your guests should then spread plum sauce on a lettuce leaf, add some chicken mince, wrap then eat. If you have oriental bowls use them for this dish.

Lemon Chicken and Rosemary Roast Potatoes

Preparation & cooking time: 55 minutes
Serves 4

I am sure you will love these flavours as the rosemary, garlic and lemon work so well together. It's a very easy entertaining dish as once you have prepared it, all you have to do is place it in the oven when your guests arrive.

5 potatoes
1 large chicken
6 lemons
4 cloves of garlic
3 tablespoons honey
Fresh rosemary
2 tablespoons olive oil

Start by jointing the chicken into 4 large pieces plus the two wings. In a large frying pan heat half a tablespoon of olive oil and fry half the chicken. Remove the chicken after you have sealed all sides (this should take 2 minutes on each side). Add another half tablespoon of olive oil and fry the remaining chicken.

Squeeze all the lemon juice into a casserole and keep the lemons aside. Crush the garlic and mix with the lemon juice followed by the honey. Mix well so that the honey dissolves. Add the chicken and place about six empty lemon halves between the pieces. Place in a fan assisted oven at 180°C (200°C regular) or gas mark 6 for 45 minutes.

Peel and quarter the potatoes. Boil them for just 2-3 minutes. Drain and place the potatoes in an oven dish. Drizzle over them a tablespoon of oil and season with salt and pepper. Shred the fresh rosemary with your hands over the potatoes and stir. Place the potatoes in a heated fan assisted oven on 180°C (200° regular) and cook for 35 minutes, stirring them occasionally.

Chicken Napoli

Preparation & cooking time: 30 minutes
Serves 4

Such an easy dish with no fuss. Just simple ingredients and a wonderful flavour.

4	chicken breasts
½	can pitted black olives
1	can chopped tomatoes
150ml	(¼ pint) vegetable stock
2	cloves garlic
1	tablespoon olive oil

In a large pan heat the olive oil then sear the chicken breasts (approximately 2 minutes on each side). At this point add your can of tomatoes followed by the stock. Cut the olives in halves then add to the pan. Crush the garlic into the pan and season. Simmer on a very low heat for about 20 minutes. The liquid should then be reduced into a chunky sauce.

Now you are ready to serve. A great accompaniment is warm ciabatta bread or French loaf to mop up the sauce .

Chicken Wrapped in Parma Ham with Cinnamon and Clove Chutney

Preparation & cooking time: 1 hour
Serves 4

4 skinless chicken breasts
12 slices parma ham
Handful of spinach leaves per chicken breast

For the chutney

1 450ml (16 fl.oz.) can tomatoes
1 large onion
100g (3½ oz.) brown sugar
200ml (7 fl.oz.) white wine vinegar
1 teaspoon ground cloves
1 teaspoon cinnamon
1 teaspoon salt
1 red chilli (with or without seeds)

Start by cooking the chutney. This can be done ahead of time and kept in the refrigerator. (It makes a lot and can be used at a later time). Combine all the ingredients, adding the finely chopped chilli. Cook slowly for 50-60 minutes until the sauce thickens.

Blanch the spinach leaves in boiling water or steam until they have wilted. Take a breast of chicken and make a cavity in the middle. Stuff the chicken breasts with spinach and wrap each in 3 slices of parma ham so they are completely sealed. Place on a rack (for any fat to drip off) over a baking tray in a preheated fan assisted oven at 200°C (220°C regular) or gas mark 7 and cook for 20 minutes. When the chicken is ready, slice into 2 inch wheels . Place 3-4 slices on each plate, add a spoonful of chutney and serve.

This dish goes perfectly with mashed potato mixed with a teaspoon of pommery mustard, the grainy variety.

Low Fat Tandoori Chicken

Preparation & cooking time: 40 minutes
Serves 4

8	chicken breasts, skinned
3	garlic cloves, crushed
2cm	(1 in.) piece fresh ginger
2	small red chillies
600ml	(1 pint) low fat yoghurt
1	tablespoon ground coriander
2	teaspoons tandoori or curry paste
	Handful fresh coriander chopped

There are many ways to adapt Indian cuisine to low fat cooking. Here is a perfect example.

For the marinade, chop finely the ginger and chilli. Mix together adding the crushed garlic. Pour in the yoghurt, ground spices and curry paste and combine well. Add the fresh coriander and give another mix.

Make three cuts on each chicken breast going about half an inch into the flesh. This will help collect all the flavour while cooking. Put the chicken into the marinade and leave in the refrigerator for a few hours to enhance the flavours.

When ready, turn on your grill and when it's really hot, place the chicken breasts on a tray and cook for about 25 minutes. If you have any marinade left in the bowl, baste the chicken half way through the cooking.

Let the chicken go really brown. Serve on steamed plain rice to soak up all the great juices.

Thai Basil Chicken

Preparation & cooking time: 15 minutes
Serves 4

Chicken does not get better than this or more simple. If you have been to Thailand, make this and bring all the smells and wonderful tastes back home with you. This is great to make in large portions to keep in the fridge as the flavours just get better with time.

450g (1 lb.) ground chicken
4 cloves garlic
4 spring onions, chopped
1 teaspoon sesame oil
4 small red chillies, finely chopped
¾ cup basil leaves, chopped
2 tablespoons fish sauce

Heat a wok, add oil and stir fry the garlic and spring onions until tender but not browned, about 1-2 minutes. Add chilli peppers and stir for about 1 minute more. Throw in the chicken mince and stir fry until cooked through. Add the basil and fish sauce. Mix thoroughly and serve over rice if desired.

Thai Red Curry

Preparation & cooking time: 25 minutes
Serves 4

I have worked very hard to make curries fat free and I think I have cracked it. If you want to make this curry creamier you can add a drizzle of low fat coconut cream. I make this really spicy but will leave it to you on how hot you make it.

450g (1 lb.) beef, cubed (sliced steak works well)
1 large onion finely chopped
100ml (3.5 fl.oz.) vegetable stock (from a cube is fine)
2 cloves crushed garlic
2.5cm (1 in.) piece fresh ginger, grated
1 tablespoon Thai red curry paste
2 chillies minimum
200g (7 oz.) mixed vegetables (broccoli, cauliflower, beans etc)
Handful fresh coriander

In a large non stick pan or wok heat and fry the beef. Add the onion and vegetables followed by the garlic, chillies and curry paste. Stir well and lower the heat then add the stock followed by the ginger. Cover and simmer for 15 minutes on a low heat. Throw in the coriander, roughly chopped, and serve.

Low Fat Chicken Curry

Preparation & cooking time: 25 minutes
Serves 4

Curries are renowned for being high in fat so I have developed a fat free version. It's my best invention yet and is so powerful in flavour. Try it with salmon or cod if you are tired of chicken. If you make this curry, I'm sure you'll experiment to find your own favourite version.

4 chicken breasts
1 large onion finely chopped
100ml (3½ fl.oz.) vegetable stock (from a cube is fine)
2 cloves crushed garlic
2.5cm (1 in.) piece fresh ginger, grated
1 -2 tablespoons curry powder
2 chillies or as many as you wish
200g (7 oz.) mixed vegetables (e.g. broccoli, cauliflower, beans)
Handful fresh coriander

In a large non stick pan or wok fry the chicken breasts until brown (you can do this with a little oil if you like). Add onion and vegetables followed by the garlic, chillies and curry powder. Mix and lower heat then add stock followed by the grated ginger. Mix well and cover for 15 minutes on a low heat. Add more stock if needed. Just before serving throw in roughly chopped coriander.

Moroccan Lamb Steaks on Cous Cous

Preparation & cooking time: 15-20 minutes
Serves 4

Ideal for a summer's evening dinner party.

4 large lamb steaks (boneless)
3 cups cous cous
1 lemon
4 spring onions
1 cup french beans

For the marinade

1 tablespoon soy sauce
1 teaspoon honey
Drop of olive oil
1 clove crushed garlic
Fresh rosemary finely chopped
Juice of 1 lemon

Start by marinating the lamb. Add all the marinade ingredients to a large bowl and add the lamb steaks to this, cutting each one into three pieces. Refrigerate for at least an hour to absorb the flavours.

Place the cous cous in a bowl and cover with boiling water just above the level of the cous cous. Cover with a plate for 5 minutes. Boil the beans, chop and add to the cous cous with the juice of one lemon and chopped spring onions. Fluff the cous cous with a fork and place a few spoonfuls on each plate.

You will now need to fry the lamb but if you have a griddle pan use it, as it gives the markings of a barbecue and you need not use any oil. This will take a few minutes on each side depending how well done you like the lamb. Just before the lamb is ready, spoon over the remaining marinade then serve over the cous cous.

Spicy Beef Burgers

Preparation & cooking time: 15-18 minutes
Serves 4

450g	(1 lb.) lean beef mince
2	garlic cloves, crushed
1	red chilli
	Handful fresh basil Leaves
1	small onion
2	spring onions
1	egg
1	teaspoon mustard
1	teaspoon tomato ketchup

This is perfect on a grill or barbecue and you can adapt this with lamb mince or chicken.

In a large bowl mix together the mince, garlic, tomato ketchup, mustard, egg and the chilli finely chopped. Finely dice the onion and add to the beef. I find the best way to mix this is by hand. Dive in with your hands and mix until the ingredients are well blended. If you prepare the mix a day before the flavours will intensify.

Before cooking, slice the spring onions and basil and mix with the beef. In a large non stick frying pan add a little olive oil and fry the beef mix in burger size portions. Turn them once only, frying 5-6 minutes each side. Alternatively you can cook under a grill for the same time turning half way through.

Serve with burger buns or with a salad.

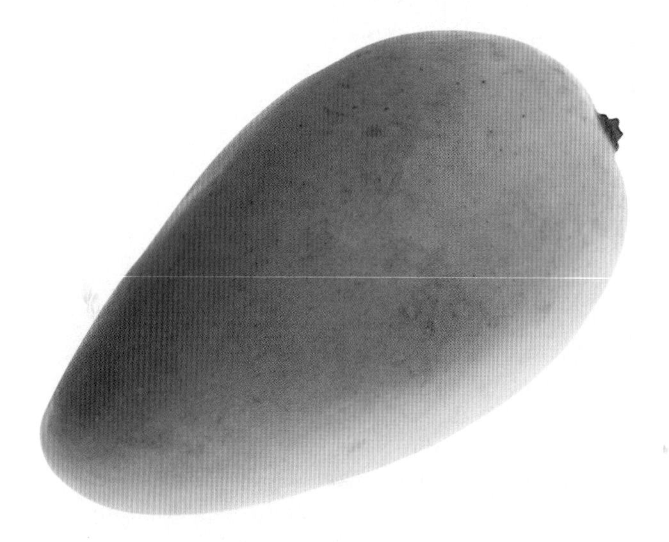

A Sweet Ending But Still Low Fat

Sesame Bananas

Fruit Smoothie

Asian Summer Pudding

Crepes with Mango, Lychee, Palm Sugar and Lime

Mango Sorbet

Tropical Fruit Salad with Raspberry Coulis

Sesame Bananas

Preparation & cooking time: 15-18 minutes
Serves 4

4	ripe bananas
1	lemon
2	tablespoons white sesame seeds
4	tablespoons water
110g	(4 oz.) sugar

This is a perfect end to a dinner party as most guests have eaten well and do not wish for a heavy dessert. It's so simple but again gives a hint of the East.

Cut each banana into 4 or 5 slices. Cut them at an angle purely for presentation. Place them in a bowl and squeeze the juice of the lemon over them. This will stop them from turning brown. Transfer the bananas to a serving dish.

In a pan, bring the water and sugar to the boil and simmer until it reduces to a thick liquid. Quickly so it does not go hard, drizzle over the banana pieces. Sprinkle with the sesame seeds and serve immediately or let stand for a while.

If you want to serve this with an accompaniment, mix some low fat fromage frais or plain yoghurt with sugar and cinnamon to have on the side.

Fruit Smoothie

Preparation time: 8-10 minutes
Serves 4

2 bananas
200g (7 oz.) strawberries
200g (7 oz.) low fat plain yoghurt
1 tablespoon honey
1 teaspoon cinnamon
1 teaspoon brown sugar
450ml (¾ pint) fat free milk
300ml (½ pint) orange juice

So easy and so fresh. This recipe really should be taken as a guideline for you to adapt to your taste. Use any fruit you like and add different juices too. Experiment: you will not go wrong. All you do is blend all the ingredients until smooth. Keep in the fridge and serve over ice. If you are serving straight away add ice to the blender and make more of a milk shake.

Asian Summer Pudding

Preparation time: 8-10 minutes
Serves 4

6	slices white bread, crusts removed
100ml	(3.5 fl.oz.) orange juice
250g	(9 oz.) strawberries
1	large mango
10-15	lychee
1	large papaya
1	tablespoon sugar

This is adapted from the English summer pudding that uses seasonal berries and sugar. I have adapted it for Asian fruits.

Either take a cake tin or as I prefer for presentation, four ramekin dishes or timbales. Blend the strawberries to a pulp in a blender. Place the orange juice, sugar and strawberry mix in a pan and heat long enough for them to dissolve together. Dip the bread in the mixture and line your dish or dishes with it.

Cut the remaining fruit into small cubes and mix together. Fill the bread mould with the fruit. Save a slice of bread to place on top of the pudding. You can use an extra slice for this if required.

Put the pudding in the refrigerator and serve chilled. Garnish the pudding with whatever takes your fancy.

If you have any liquid left over from the orange juice and strawberries, drizzle over your serving plate.

Crepes with Mango, Lychee, Palm Sugar and Lime

Preparation & cooking time: 20 minutes
Serves 4

For the crepes
110g (4 oz.) plain four
2 eggs
200ml (7 fl.oz.) semi or skimmed milk

For the filling
1 large mango
10-15 lychee
3 limes
Palm sugar

I have always loved making crepes from childhood and now I have sophisticated the taste from the original lemon and sugar tradition.

First, make the crepe batter. Sieve the flour and make a well in the middle. Add the eggs and start to whisk. Pour a little of the milk at a time and whisk until you have a smooth mixture with no lumps.

Chop the mango into cubes, chop the lychee and mix the fruits together.

In a non-stick pan add a tiny drizzle of oil. When the pan is very hot turn down the heat to a more moderate temperature. Ladle a thin layer of crepe batter into the pan, just coating it. When you see bubbles appear on the surface the crepe is ready to flip over. Cook for another minute on the other side. I do not know why but the first crepe never turns out well. I think it's an adjustment of the heat.

Onto each crepe add some fruit followed by sugar and a good squeeze of lime. Roll up the crepe and serve.

I have not stated the amount of sugar to be used as I feel it is up to the taste of the individual. I think a teaspoon is plenty per crepe as you have such delicious rich sweet fruits.

Mango Sorbet

Preparation: 15-20 minutes. Freezing: 2 hours minimum
Serves 4

2	medium mangoes
3	tablespoons sugar
1	egg white whisked until stiff
	Juice of 1 lemon

Sorbet is so easy to make. Try this dish once and then use you favourite fruits to make exciting combinations.

In a saucepan dissolve the sugar in 150ml (5 fl.oz.) of water. Bring to the boil and cook until syrupy, stirring constantly. Leave to cool.

Puree the mango and stir in the egg white and lemon juice. Stir into the cooled syrup. Place in the freezer to set.

I like to freeze in individual serving bowls for my guests.

Tropical Fruit Salad with Raspberry Coulis

Preparation time: 10 minutes
Serves 4

1	large mango
1	dragon fruit (if available)
1	melon (any type)
12	strawberries

For the coulis

225g	(½ lb.) raspberries
2	tablespoons icing sugar

Dragon fruit is a spectacular looking fruit and looks great in any fruit salad. Use the fruit I have chosen as a guideline. Choose whatever takes your fancy or that is in season. The way I make this more interesting is by using the coulis.

All you do is divide the fruit into 4 portions and put the raspberries in a blender along with the icing sugar and blend to a pulp. Place a little coulis at the base of each glass then add some fruit, pour the remaining coulis over each glass.

Index

T

W